Modern World Religions

Islam

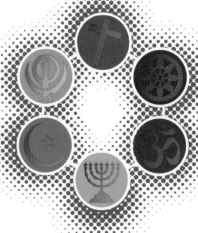

Andrew Egan

Heinemann

For Olivia

Heinemann is an imprint of Pearson Education Limited, a company incorporated in England and Wales, having its registered office at Edinburgh Gate, Harlow, Essex, CM20 2JE. Registered company number: 872828

Heinemann is a registered trademark of Pearson Education Limited

First published in 2002

08
10 9 8

British Library Cataloguing in Publication Data
A catalogue record for this book is available from the British Library

ISBN: 978 0 435336 11 0

Picture research by Jennifer Johnson
Designed and typeset by Artistix, Thame, Oxon
Printed and bound in China (CTPS/08)

Acknowledgements
The author would like to thank Imam Aurangzeb Khan for all the wise words and kind prayers that have helped to make this book possible.

The publishers would like to thank the following for permission to use photographs:

Andes Press Agency/Carlos Reyes-Mayer, p. 45; Andes Press Agency/D&C Hill, p. 52; Andrew Egan, p. 8; Hutchison Picture Library/Edward Parker, p. 44; Hutchison Picture Library/Nigel Smith, p. 42; Hutchison Picture Library/Titus Moser, p. 15; Panos Pictures/Jeremy Hartley, pp. 47 and 48; Panos Pictures/Penny Tweedie, p. 51; Rex Features/Eastlight Vienna, p. 55; Science Photo Library/Celestial Image Co., p. 57; Science Photo Library/ESA/Photo Library International, p. 40; Science Photo Library/Peter Menzel, p. 56. All other photographs supplied by Peter Sanders.

The publishers have made every effort to contact copyright holders. However, if any material has been incorrectly acknowledged, the publishers would be pleased to correct this at the earliest opportunity.

Tel: 01865 888058   www.heinemann.co.uk

Contents

An introduction to Islam

In this section you will:
- develop an understanding of the nature and importance of faith and trust
- think about the ways in which Islam seeks to strengthen faith in Allah
- express your own views on the aims of Islam.

Standing before Allah in prayer

Faith and trust

The religion of **Islam**, like all religions, is based on **belief**. To believe in something means that you have no doubt at all, even if there is very little evidence to back up your belief.

To believe in something requires **faith** and **trust**. Faith is often seen as the courage to accept the challenges of belief and trust as the certainty that you won't be let down.

The people who follow Islam are called **Muslims**. The worldwide community of Muslims is known as the **ummah**. The ummah shows Islam to be one great family, different in local culture and custom, but still united as one family before Allah.

Islam teaches that no one is superior to another except if one is more faithful to Allah. Islam aims at the development of an united human society on earth guided by the holy laws of Allah.

Allah

All Muslims have faith and trust in **Allah**, the Almighty God who created all things. For Muslims, Islam is more than just a series of beliefs, it is a complete way of life. They believe that not only has Allah created all things but that Allah has also provided guidance to help all people live good lives. Therefore to be a true Muslim means to accept Allah as the one true God and to submit to His will.

A Muslim family

The aims of Islam

Islam grants freedom of thought to all believers. It strives to free the soul from sin and wrong and to strengthen it with goodness and purity. This is so that people can live lives dedicated to doing their best in the eyes of Allah, on behalf of other people and for themselves. Islam also aims to free the human self from vanity and greed, from envy and tension, from fear and insecurity. Islam, through submission to Allah, seeks to free people from the worship of false gods and low desires, unfolding before them the beautiful horizons of goodness and excellence. Islam fills the heart with fear of Allah, the only God in this world as well as the hereafter.

Islam wants to see its followers as honest, dutiful, pious, kind-hearted, reliable and sincere; this is achieved by a system of worship and duties.

Muslims are certain of their faith because Allah has told people about Himself over the centuries through holy people known as **prophets**. This is called revelation as Allah has used prophets to reveal something of Himself to people. The **Qur'an**, the Muslim holy book, mentions by name 25 prophets of Allah beginning with **Adam (pbuh)** and finishing with **Muhammad** (pbuh).

To show deep respect to the prophets of Islam, Muslims will say 'peace be upon him' when mentioning a prophet by name. Throughout this book (pbuh) will appear as a sign of respect after the mention of the names of any of the prophets of Allah. For Muslims, the last and greatest of the prophets was Muhammad (pbuh) to whom Allah revealed the Qur'an, His final message for the guidance of all.

Learning about religion

❶ a Discuss with a partner what you understand by the words 'faith' and 'trust'.

 b Jot your thoughts down in rough and share them with your class.

 c Write up the definitions that you are happy with.

❷ a How do faith and trust strengthen belief in Allah for Muslims?

 b Why it is fair to say that Islam is a religion built upon these two principles?

❸ a List carefully what you consider to be the main aims of Islam.

 b As you progress through the units in this textbook, add to your list as you find out more about the faith of Islam.

Learning from religion

❶ a Is there anything or anyone you could say you trusted or had faith in?

 b Why have you chosen them?

❷ Why do you think it is important for people to have faith in their lives?

❸ Do you think the world would be a very different place if no one showed any trust?

The prophet Muhammad (pbuh)

In this section you will:

- find out about the vocation/calling of the prophet Muhammad (pbuh)
- begin to understand the nature of the message Muhammad (pbuh) was to convey to the people of Makkah
- reflect on how you might think Muhammad (pbuh) would have felt as he began his mission.

Muhammad's (pbuh) childhood

The prophet **Muhammad** (**pbuh**) was born in **Makkah** in 569 CE. Makkah is now in the modern country of Saudi Arabia.

By the time he was eight, his parents and grandparents were dead. He went into the care of his uncle, **Abu Talib**, a man who was kind and generous. Abu Talib travelled the region meeting many different people and doing business with them. Muhammad (pbuh) would often accompany his uncle on his business journeys.

The prophet of Islam

The people of Makkah were very superstitious and had little understanding of who **Allah** was, so they put their faith in statues and lucky charms. Muhammad (pbuh) was not like the others. He was a man of deep faith and prayed regularly. Gradually his spiritual meditation grew deeper and deeper. He would often isolate himself in a cave on **Jabal-un-Nur** (the Mountain of Light). There he would pray and meditate and share what little food he had with passers-by.

When he was 40 years old Muhammad (pbuh) was meditating one night when suddenly the Angel **Jibril** appeared before him in the cave.

The **Angel** told him that Allah had chosen him as His Final Messenger to all mankind. The Angel told him to recite (read out loud) the words on the cloth he was carrying and Muhammad (pbuh), although he could not read before that night, recited the following verses:

'In the name of Allah, Most Gracious, Most Merciful.
Recite! (read aloud): In the name of your Lord
Who has created;
He has Created man from a clot.
Recite! And your Lord is Most Generous.
Who taught by the pen,
He has taught man that which he knew not.'

Qur'an, **surah** 96: 1–5

Muhammad (pbuh) was overawed by this incident and returned home dazed. He told **Khadijah**, his wife, what had happened to him. Muhammad thought that some evil spirit might be involved. Khadijah consoled him, saying that unlike most of the people of Makkah, he had always been generous and kind and assured him that Allah would protect him against all evil.

Muhammad's (pbuh) marriage to Khadijah was important as it provided him with a firm base of love and companionship upon which to build the mission to which Allah had called him. Without the faith and trust of his most loyal partner, his task would have been all the more difficult. Soon, another revelation directed him to warn people against evil, to encourage them to worship no other gods but Allah and to give up everything that could displease Allah:

'O you enveloped in garments,
Arise and warn!
And magnify your Lord
And purify your garments and keep away from idols.
And give not a thing in order to have more
And be patient for the sake of your Lord.'

Qur'an, surah 74: 1–7

Another revelation warned him to proclaim his mission openly:

'Proclaim openly that which you are
    commanded, and
Turn away from the idolaters.
Truly We will suffice you against the scoffers.'

Qur'an, surah 15: 94–5

It was essential that the people of Makkah heard and accepted the will of Allah, changed their ways and led better lives. It was Muhammad's (pbuh) task to ensure this happened.

The chain of revelations from Allah continued until the last one came 23 years after the first:

'This day, I have perfected your religion for you and completed My Favour upon you and have chosen for you Islam as your religion.'

Qur'an, surah 5: 3

After Muhammad's (pbuh) death all the revelations that he had received from Allah were written down as the **Qur'an**, the holy book of **Islam**.

The cave above Makkah

Learning about religion

❶ The word 'vocation' means 'calling'. Do you think it is right for Muslims to claim that Muhammad (pbuh) had a vocation?

❷ Briefly describe what you consider to be the most important features of Muhammad's (pbuh) call to prophethood. Explain why you have chosen each one.

❸ What concerns do you think Muhammad (pbuh) shared with Khadijah on being called by Allah to be His Prophet?

Learning from religion

❶ What evidence is there to suggest that Muhammad (pbuh) was well suited to the office of Prophet?

❷ a Look carefully at the quotes from the Qur'an in this chapter. What aspects of Makkan religious life and practice did Allah command Muhammad (pbuh) to reform?

b What aspects of life today would you want to see changed to make for a better world? How would you deal with people who did not agree with you?

❸ Muhammad (pbuh) said, 'God does not accept beliefs if they are not expressed in deeds: and your deeds are worthless if they do not back up your beliefs'. How easy do you feel it is to simply pay lip service to religious beliefs, and not match pious words with deeds?

The prophets

In this section you will:

- explore the essential characteristics of a prophet
- understand the importance of prophethood in Islam
- evaluate the importance of the office of prophet for Muslims.

The messengers of Allah

Understanding the importance of prophethood is essential for a complete understanding of **Islam**. **Muslims** believe that **Muhammad** (**pbuh**) was the last of all the **prophets** of **Allah**.

The word 'prophethood' comes from the Arabic word '**risalah**', which means 'message'. In this case it means the communication of important news. Muslims believe that a prophet is someone who is sent by Allah to convey His message to other people.

Prophethood is not something that can be acquired by an individual's personal effort or devotion to Allah. It is Allah's special gift which He gives to a human being. There is no human involvement in His decision-making. Allah decides who is fit to be a prophet.

In the **Qur'an** this calling from Allah is called **istjfaa**, which means the selection of the best people. Muslims believe that the prophets were not like other people – they were born to be prophets and had qualities that no other human beings can have.

The message

'A prophet never speaks on his own accord Nor does he speak of (his own) desire. It is only a Revelation revealed (by Allah).'

Qur'an, **surah** 53: 3–4

Islamic name	Biblical name
1 Ādam	Adam
2 Idrīs	Enoch
3 Noh	Noah
4 Had	——
5 Sālih	——
6 Ibrāhim	Abraham
7 Ismā'il	Ishmael
8 Ishāq	Isaac
9 Lot	Lot
10 Ya'qūb	Jacob
11 Yūsuf	Joseph
12 Shu'aib	——
13 Ayyūb	Job
14 Musā	Moses
15 Harūn	Aaron
16 Dhul-Kifl	Ezekiel
17 Dāwūd	David
18 Suleimān	Solomon
19 Ilyās	Elias
20 Al Yasa'	Elisha
21 Yūnas	Jonah
22 Zakaryah	Zechariah
23 Yahyā	John
24 'Īsa	Jesus
25 Muhammad	——
(Peace be upon them all)	

The prophets of Islam

This means that Allah's message cannot be influenced by the personal thoughts or desires of a prophet. The word of Allah always remains undiluted in the hands of the prophet, while this is not possible in the case of an ordinary person. This is what distinguishes him from other human beings.

Examples of prophetic teaching include:

'He is not a believer who eats his fill while his neighbour remains hungry by his side.'

Muhammad (pbuh)

'There are many who fast during the day and pray all night, but they gain nothing but hunger and sleeplessness.'

Muhammad (pbuh)

'I say to you love God and love your neighbour as you love yourself.'

'Isa – Jesus (pbuh)

'When you fast, wash your face and look happy, that your fasting may not be seen by men but by your Father who is in secret; and your Father who is in secret will reward you.'

'Isa – Jesus (pbuh)

'The Lord is in His holy temple, the Lord's throne is in heaven; the Lord is good, He loves good deeds; the upright shall see His face.'

Dawud – David (pbuh)

'The righteous has enough to satisfy his appetite, but the belly of the wicked suffers want.'

Suleiman – Solomon (pbuh)

The message is very clear. The commandments from Allah (The Lord – Judaism, God – Christianity) demand of every individual a real sense of duty both towards Allah and towards other people.

Learning about religion

❶ 'Islam teaches that prophets are born and not made.' Do you agree with this statement? Give reasons for your decision.

❷ What do you consider to be the most important qualities required of someone holding the office of a prophet?

❸ Why do you think Islam teaches that the example and teaching of the prophets are essential for growth in faith?

Learning from religion

❶ How easy do you think it must be to accept the responsibility of a prophetic vocation? What sort of feelings and emotions would rush through a prophet when they feel Allah's call?

❷ Prophets are often thought of as lone voices telling people the way in which Allah wants them to live.

   a Do you think that there are people acting like prophets in society today? What messages are they trying to put across?

   b What might be the consequences if no one takes any notice?

❸ Like Islam, the religions of Christianity and Judaism also place great importance on the mission of the prophets. Interestingly, many prophets are held in common by all three faiths.

   a Look at the prophetic quotes above. In what ways are their messages similar? In what ways are they different?

   b Why do you think that they are both similar and different?

   c 'If people concentrated on the similarities between religions rather than the differences, the world would be a better place.' Do you agree? What reasons would you give to support your views?

Muslim leadership and authority

In this section you will:

- discover something of the role of the imam in the Muslim community
- consider the important role played by learned people in the faith of Islam
- express your own views on the nature and importance of leaders in faith communities.

The role of the imam

Many world faiths depend on the work of local religious leaders to guide them in their spiritual development and to be available to advise or comfort them in particular times of crisis or need. For example, Jews may look to their rabbi or Christians to their priest at such times. Jewish rabbis and Christian priests are often paid for the work they do as the calling to serve God that they are following is their full time occupation. The role of the **imam** in the **Muslim** community is different.

Generally speaking, in **Islam** there are no paid religious leaders. The **Qur'an** is clear in stating that Islam should not try to attract people to serve **Allah** by the promise of financial rewards.

Imam Aurangzeb Khan

'Leading a community in prayer before Allah is an honour, and teaching the meaning and importance of the word of Allah a privilege; to be paid would add nothing.

'I trained for seven years to become an imam. The training involved full study of both the Qur'an and the **Hadiths**. I felt called to this through a sense of wanting to develop my own prayer life and dedication to Allah. The honour of being asked to then help others is a great bonus. Allah has given all things, including all our feelings and emotions. One thing in particular that He has given is the ability to ask questions like who am I? where have I come from? and where am I going? in terms of my relationship with Allah. I am a child of Allah and as such I want to grow closer to Him, fully engaged in His service.

'I see my main task as being there to help others to maintain their prayer life. For me my prayer life is rather like owning a car, if you look after it and service it regularly, it will serve you well. So it is with prayer, looked after well your prayer life will flourish and serve you well for life.'

Imam Aurangzeb Khan

Although it is rare, Muslim scholars have stated that in certain circumstances where a man is dedicated and fully engaged in his work as an imam then he may receive payment.

The imam is usually chosen by the local Muslim community that he is to serve. Any Muslim of good character can be an imam providing he:

- has a good knowledge of Islam
- is respected and held in high regard by fellow Muslims
- has studied the Qur'an, the holy book of Islam and the Hadiths, the sayings of the prophet Muhammad (pbuh) in Arabic and understands them well

An imam leading worship in a mosque

● is known for his faithfulness to and love of Allah and his ability to make wise decisions based upon good judgement.

Leading prayers

The main role of the imam is to lead the prayers at the **mosque** (the local centre of Muslim worship) in his community. Before the Friday lunchtime prayers (the most important prayers of the week) the imam will give two short talks or sermons called the **khutbah**. These sermons will usually involve an explanation of verses of the Qur'an or else a consideration of the important relevance of the Hadiths for Muslims today.

Similarly, it is the imam who will often lead prayers and read a sermon at a Muslim marriage or funeral and who will take a leading role in the work of the **madrasah** or school at the mosque where young Muslims will go to study Islam and in particular to study the Qur'an and to learn Arabic.

It is essential to remember that the imam is not a leader of Muslims. Islam is a faith that allows all its followers the space to find and to worship Allah for themselves. No Muslim, however learned or pious, would ever feel it right to tell another what to do or how to live their lives, because ultimately we are all answerable to Allah alone as individuals. The imam will, however, always encourage all in his community to live their lives in accordance with Islamic teachings.

Learning about religion

❶ Briefly describe the nature and importance of the work of the imam in a Muslim community.

❷ Read the quotation from Imam Aurangzeb Khan. Explain how these words can help non-Muslims to understand the role of the imam.

Learning from religion

❶ Many religious communities rely on professional religious leaders such as priests or rabbis.

　a　Why do you think this is so? What difference can such leaders make to the life of a faith community, for example through their work in the Christian church or the Jewish synagogue?

　b　Consider reasons why Islam has no such professional religious leaders.

　c　What similarities and differences do you think would exist between communities that have professional leaders and those that do not? Give reasons for your answers.

❷ What do you think are the benefits of religions:

　a　having leaders

　b　not having leaders?

　　Share your thoughts with a neighbour before writing down your responses as fully as possible.

Muslim beliefs

In this section you will:

- find out about the most important Muslim beliefs
- analyze the impact of these beliefs on both individuals and communities.

Muslims believe that the religion of **Islam**, revealed to the **prophet Muhammad** (**pbuh**), is the true religion of **Allah**, the one true God. The most fundamental **beliefs** of Islam are:

1 in Allah

2 in the will of Allah (predestination)

3 in the angels of Allah

4 in the books of Allah

5 in the messengers (prophets) of Allah

6 in the day of judgement

7 in life after death.

These seven fundamental beliefs can be placed into three broader groups:

1 **tawhid** – the oneness of Allah

2 **risalah** – the work and message of the prophets

3 **akhirah** – life after death.

Tawhid, risalah and akhirah summarize the whole of the Muslim way of life.

Tawhid

Tawhid means the oneness of Allah. It is the main part of the faith of Muslims and is expressed most beautifully in the **Qur'an**:

'Say, He is Allah, the One. Allah is the self sufficient master Whom all creatures need. He begets not nor was begotten. And there is none co-equal or comparable to Him.'

Qur'an, **surah** 112

Tawhid means that everything on earth is created by Allah. It is Allah who is therefore the sustainer of the universe and the only source of human guidance.

'It is Allah alone who has created all things, given all things, is all things. We would have nothing, be nothing without Allah.'

Mariah, aged 14

Risalah

Risalah refers to the important role played by the prophets in Islam.

'Allah sent among them a messenger from among themselves, reciting unto them His Verses, and purifying them, and instructing them in the book and wisdom.'

Qur'an, surah 3: 164

2

3. ANGELS OF ALLAH
4. BOOKS OF ALLAH
5. MESSENGERS OF ALLAH

RISALAH

1

1. ALLAH
2. PREDESTINATION

TAWHID

3

6. DAY OF JUDGEMENT
7. LIFE AFTER DEATH

AKHIRAH

This means quite simply that:

'Allah has sent His messenger with … the religion of truth, to make it victorious.'

Qur'an, surah 61: 9

'Allah wants to guide us when we go wrong or help us when we misunderstand. For me, the prophets are those specially chosen by Allah to guide and help us to know Allah better and to understand what Allah wants.'

Mudassir, aged 15

Akhirah

Akhirah refers to the important Muslim belief in a life after death that can be enjoyed by all believers. Allah's message is:

'Did you think that We had created you in play and that you would not be brought back to us?'

Qur'an, surah 23: 115

'And those who disbelieve say "when we have become dust we and our fathers, shall we really be brought forth again?"'

Qur'an, surah 27: 67

This is because those who disbelieve deny that there is life after death. For Muslims, however, the answer to the question 'is there life after death' is a definite 'yes', because Allah has promised a glorious afterlife and Allah never breaks His promises.

'Life does not simply begin when we are physically born and end when we physically die. Really our lives belonging to Allah begin before physical birth and continue after physical death. This is really simple to understand when you think of every human life as belonging to Allah.'

Mudassir, aged 15

In effect, then, Islam teaches that human life is one eternal life made up of two parts, life before and life after death. Muslims believe that the spirit of life that Allah has breathed into everyone is raised by Allah, from death to the afterlife. It is to be here, in the afterlife, that Allah will call all to account for themselves and judge them according to the way they have led their lives on earth. Those who have led good lives, it is said, will enter paradise with Allah and those who have led bad, wicked lives will be punished.

Learning about religion

❶ In pairs prepare a short speech in which you and your partner explain the meaning and importance of tawhid, risalah and akhirah to your class. Devise your own diagrams to help you get across what you want to say.

❷ In your opinion are tawhid, risalah and akhirah all of equal importance to understanding Islam, or are they different? Think carefully about your answer and support it with reasons.

Learning from religion

❶ What difference do you think belief in tawhid, risalah and akhirah makes in the daily lives of Muslim people and communities?

❷ Look at the quotations from the Muslim children on these pages. Explain carefully the importance Islam plays in their lives. Why do you think this is so? What evidence from the quotations would you use to support your answers?

❸ How would you explain the Muslim concept of life after death?

Allah

In this section you will:

- develop an understanding of the most important characteristics of Allah
- think about how you would describe God
- share your thoughts about God in a variety of ways.

Muslim beliefs about Allah

Some people seem to pass their entire lives without ever thinking about the reason for their existence, or whether there is any point to their lives, or any goal to be aimed for. Many think there is a universe and that is all there is. They believe their lives are simply a chain of events until they die.

Muslims, however, say it is impossible for anything to have being or purpose without God. To recognize that **Allah** does exist and is the beginning and end of all things is essential to the **faith** of **Islam**.

Muslims believe that Allah is one and at one with all things and that there is no other god except Him. This belief is called **tawhid**. The **prophet Muhammad** (**pbuh**) attacked all forms of **belief** in God which denied His oneness and unity.

The word 'Islam' means 'submission'. The way in which Muslims submit themselves to the will of Allah accurately reflects what Muslims believe about Allah and the way in which Allah expects them to live their lives. True Muslims would never put themselves and what they want first but reflect on what Allah would expect and obey His will.

Allah, the name of God

Shirk

Blasphemy means acting or speaking disrespectfully about God. The Arabic word **shirk** can be understood as describing a form of blasphemy.

Shirk can be thought of as the blasphemy of 'association', that is to say, to talk or act in any way which denies that Allah is Lord over everything by associating Him with someone or something else. Anyone who does this commits the most awful blasphemy. The name 'Allah' in Arabic – the language of the **Qur'an** – has no plural form, and is neither male nor female. Shirk, then, is either the worship of anything other than Allah, or the association of Allah with anything other than Allah.

Why do you think Muslims might feel the power of Allah is displayed in this sunrise?

Understanding Allah

Muslims often find it possible to understand Allah best in terms of the wonders of His creation. The whole universe is Allah's creation and everything in it belongs to Allah and is dependent on Allah.

'Allah alone created all things, gave all things, is all things. Allah is like nothing or no one, Allah is greater than anything we can ever hope to imagine, it's pointless and wrong to ever try to bring Allah down to our level. The love and power of Allah is a beautiful mystery, I'm happy with that.'

Mariah, aged 14

One of the best ways of understanding the power of Allah in the universe is through an appreciation of the light that Allah has provided for the world. The following quotations show how important the gift of light is for Muslims.

'Allah will give you a Light by which you will walk.'

Qur'an, **surah** 57: 28

'O Lord! Illuminate my heart with light, my sight with light and my hearing with light. Let there be light on my right hand and on my left and light behind me and light going before me.'

A prayer of Muhammad (pbuh)

'O God, who knows the innermost secrets of our hearts – lead us out of the darkness into the light.'

A prayer of Muhammad (pbuh)

Learning about religion

❶ What do you think Muslims understand by the term 'the oneness and unity of Allah'?

❷ What is meant by 'blasphemy'? Why do you think Muslims consider it so bad to blaspheme?

❸ Why do you think it is essential for all Muslims to completely submit themselves to the will of Allah?

Learning from religion

❶ Why do you think some people never think about God, or seem to make time for God in their lives?

❷ Using the quotes on this page:

   a consider the different ways in which Allah provides 'light' for Muslims

   b explain whether you think that light is a good way of explaining what God is like?

   c are there any other things in nature which might lead you to believe in the power of God?

❸ Look at the picture of the sunrise.

   a Why do you think Muslims feel that the power of Allah is displayed in such a scene?

   b How do you see God's power displayed in nature?

   c Compare your views with those of the Muslim faith. How are they similar? How are they different?

Thinking about Allah

In this section you will:

● consider reasons why it is not always easy to talk about Allah

● develop language that will enable you to reflect on the nature and being of Allah.

Madrasah – ' Muslim children learning ways to effectively express their beliefs about Allah'

The nature of the universe

For some people understanding the nature of **Allah** (God) is difficult. People have traditionally tended to think of Allah as being 'up there'

A 3-storey depiction of the universe

inhabiting a wonderful place called Heaven, surrounded by His **angels** and all the good people who have died and gone to glory. The opposite can be said for **Shaytan** (the Devil) who dwells far beneath the earth in Hell, surrounded by the forces of evil and all the wicked people who are being punished for their sins after their death. This means that we as human beings inhabit a sort of middle ground, called earth.

However, we now know scientifically that the universe in which we live is not like that. We know from all the many space missions that have been launched that the sky does not provide a home for Allah, but rather, by its many layers, gives protection for the earth from the sun's harmful rays. We also now know that the earth is round, so Hell cannot be below the earth, as that would actually be sky for people living on the other side of the world.

The nature of Allah

Muslims prefer to talk of Allah as being one absolute power. The absolute power of Allah is plain for all to see. The laws of nature, the order of the universe and the beauty of creation reflect a little of Allah but are not Allah. Allah is above and beyond the universe, unlimited by time and space. He knows everything and is the all-powerful creator and controller of all things.

The beauty of Allah's creation

To make talking of Allah easier, Muslims often refer to Allah as 'He' or things belonging to Allah as 'His'. This is not to suggest that Allah is male or to deny that Allah is female, but it enables human beings, who can only have a limited understanding of Allah and a limited vocabulary, an opportunity to express feelings, prayer and other forms of worship.

The 99 names of Allah

Learning about religion

❶ Muslims believe that it is both important and necessary to talk about Allah. Why do you think that this is so?

❷ Despite the need to talk about Allah, many Muslims say that it is difficult to do so effectively. Explain why this is so.

❸ To talk about Allah, Muslims have collected the 99 names or characteristics (above) which are used to describe aspects of Allah in the Qur'an.

  a Why do you think these names can only describe 'aspects' of Allah and not Allah entirely?

  b Find out about some of the names or attributes of Allah and say why you feel they have been chosen.

Learning from religion

❶ Look carefully at the concepts of 'God' below, and reflect on the way in which 'God' is being described:

  ● 'Hear O Israel, the Lord your God the Lord is one' (Judaism)

  ● 'Baptize them in the name of God the Father, the Son and the Holy Spirit' (Christianity).

  In what ways are these descriptions similar to the Muslim 99 names for Allah? In what ways are they different?

❷ From the 99 names identify any characteristics or attributes that match most closely and/or contrast most strongly with your own understanding of 'God'.

❸ Do you feel that there is an important place for Allah/God in today's world? Explain your views carefully.

Signs and symbols

In this section you will:

- consider reasons why symbolic language is often an important part of religious belief and practice
- investigate why religious language is sometimes difficult
- evaluate the appropriateness of the star and crescent moon as symbols of Islam.

Muslims feel little need for symbols in their religion. However, as a reminder of the guidance **Allah** provides for His people, two very powerful symbols are often used in **Islam**.

The star and crescent moon

Islam began in the desert of Arabia amongst nomadic farmers who would travel by night, away from the searing heat of the sun's rays, in search of the best food and water for their animals. The moon would provide light through the darkness of the night and the stars gave fixed points which the people could use to navigate the vast desert. In just the same way, Muslims are happy to think of Allah as the great guiding light in their lives.

Islam teaches that Allah has revealed the truth through the **prophet Muhammad (pbuh)** as a guide for life, for all humanity, for all time. The star and crescent moon provide a reminder of both the permanence and the benefits of the Word and Will of Allah.

'Allah is the Spirit, the power behind all things, Allah is in all things, Allah is all things.'

Salim, aged 13

'I know that Allah loves all that He has made. Best of all Allah loves us so we return love in worship.'

Mariah, aged 14

'Allah is every mystery and every answer in the universe.'

Mudassir, aged 15

Religious language

The need for symbolic language in religion is important. When you think of it, we expect our language to cover a vast range of different jobs. Sometimes it may be used to portray feelings of love or other emotions. At other times it may be used to teach complex mathematics, comfort an upset child or negotiate a business deal. We require our language to cover a wide range of emotions and situations. Unfortunately, we only have a limited vocabulary and so tend to use the same word for a variety of meanings. For example the word 'love':

1. Olivia loves strawberries.
2. Olivia loves her Mum and Dad.
3. Olivia loves her cuddly Teddy Bear.

It is not easy to gain an exact understanding of a word as popular as 'love' as it can mean different things to different people at different times.

When people want to talk about God they have to use the same words that are commonly used in everyday language. There is a problem therefore, in what is meant exactly by the claims 'God is good' or 'God loves us'. Possible answers to this problem might be to say that:

1 a religious language, talk about God, is used in a special way as it is describing something unique

   b religious language is used in a very specific sense and should not be confused with the everyday language of the home, school and playground

2 it is because of the difficulties presented by the use of everyday words to express religious truths that:

   a symbols – pictures with a powerful meaning

   b analogies, 'symbolic pictures' – 'drawn' with words describing what something could be said to be like. For example, 'Allah's love for us is like the love of a parent for their child'

   c myths – stories which share with the reader important religious truths

are used widely by people of many religions to express their beliefs about God.

Learning about religion

❶ All around us we see pictures used as signs and symbols, at home, at school and around our town or village. Why are pictures used as signs and symbols? Why not just use words?

❷ The star and crescent moon are thought of as symbols of Islam.

   a Why are they symbols rather than signs?

   b Explain why they are effective symbols of the way in which Muslims perceive Allah.

   c Consider reasons to support the claim that Islam has no real need for any other symbols.

❸ Read the quotations on page 16.

   a Which of Allah's attributes mentioned do you think is best described as symbolic?

   b Which do you feel symbolizes best the presence of Allah in the world?

Learning from religion

❶ With a partner, discuss the things listed on page 16 that 'Olivia loves'.

   a What do you think is meant by the use of 'love' in each of the three statements?

   b Why does this suggest that we have a problem with the limitations of our vocabulary?

   c How does this problem affect talk about God? Write down your thoughts.

❷ In what ways would you agree that religious language is special and unique? In what ways would you disagree? What are your reasons?

❸ Find out more about the use and importance of symbol, analogy and myth. Explain the concept 'God is love' using:

   a a symbol

   b an analogy

   c a myth.

Worship – Shahadah

In this section you will:
- explain the importance of worshipping Allah for every Muslim
- understand the importance of **shahadah** in the worship of Allah
- express your own views on the significance of worship in Islam.

The five pillars of Islam

The most important duty of every **Muslim** is to worship **Allah**. The word 'worship' in English comes from a very old word meaning 'to give worth'. It is clear in this case that Allah is 'worth' a great deal of praise and adoration, indeed worthy of and demanding the complete submission of His people to His will.

Worshipping Allah, then, demands the total obedience of every Muslim to follow His commands and to do His will. The Arabic word for such obedience in worship is **ibadah**. Ibadah comes from the Arabic word **abd**, which means servant or slave. A servant or slave is someone who is completely obedient to their master. Every Muslim would happily admit that Allah alone is their Lord and master.

'It is then as Allah's servant or slave that a Muslim tries to live their life. In doing so every aspect of their life is the worship of Allah, from working to relaxing, from praying to raising a family.'

Imam Aurangzeb Khan

There are five duties that are of fundamental importance in Muslim worship. These five duties, often referred to as 'pillars', include:

1. **shahadah** – the declaration of faith in Allah
2. **salah** – prayer five times each day
3. **zakah** – the giving of money for the poor
4. **sawm** – fasting during the month of Ramadan
5. **Hajj** – pilgrimage to **Makkah** at least once in a lifetime.

Shahadah

The first and most important duty of every Muslim is to declare their faith in Allah. **Islam** teaches that to make this declaration a person must proclaim with their lips and believe in their heart:

'Ash hadu an laa ilaha il-allahu wa Ash hada anna Muhammadar abduhu wa rasulu.'
('I believe there is no god but Allah; and I believe that Muhammad is the servant and messenger of Allah.')

It is clear that the first part of this declaration has two aspects, one positive and one negative. 'There is no other god' is the negative aspect, 'but Allah' the positive aspect affirming the truth and certainty of Allah.

The saying of these Arabic words is called shahadah, the declaration of faith. The shahadah is repeated by Muslims every day as they wake up and just before sleeping. The words form the heart of the Muslim call to prayer (the **adhan**), used to summon Muslims to prayer five times each day. The call to prayer is also the first words whispered into the ear of a new born baby. Similarly, the last words uttered by a Muslim before dying should ideally be the **Kalimah Tayyibah**, which like the call to prayer summarizes the Muslim belief that Allah is one and that **Muhammad** (**pbuh**) is his servant and messenger.

'The message of Islam is very important and very simple, because if Allah wants you to do something He lets you know. The Prophet has taught that Allah wants worship, our way of thanking Him for everything. This worship is in the five pillars. You make a choice, to follow and worship Allah or not. It's a way of choosing either Heaven (being with Allah) or Hell (being separated from Allah).

'Islam means to submit yourself, give in to Allah. Worshipping Allah involves time and commitment throughout your life. It is right to worship, look at everything we have been given by Allah.'

Shamira, aged 13

Learning about religion

1 **a** Using the quotations from Shamira as evidence explain why she is able to claim that the message is both simple and yet very important.

   b How would the choices facing Muslims affect the way Shamira tries to live her life?

   c What difficulties might she encounter as a Muslim attending a non-Muslim school? How might these difficulties be overcome?

Learning from religion

1 **a** Imagine that as a practising Muslim student you have been asked to write a short article that explains the nature and importance of the worship of Allah for you and your family. Make sure you include an explanation of how you feel about each duty or pillar.

   b Build up the information for your article over the next few lessons as you find out more about Muslim worship.

2 'Islam is like a spiritual umbrella protecting and developing the world-wide ummah or community.' (Mamood, aged 14)

   a What evidence is there so far in your understanding of the duties of ibadah to support this view?

   b From your knowledge of Islam so far would you want to suggest that there was anything more important than the worship of Allah in the lives of Muslims? Give reasons for your answers.

3 It is interesting to note that the Shahadah is made up of two key elements, one positive and one negative.

   a Copy out the words of the shahadah. Highlight in different colours the positive and negative aspects.

   b Why do you think Muslims find understanding the positive and negative aspects of the shahadah helpful in understanding the most important aspects of faith?

Worship – Salah 1

In this section you will:

● develop an understanding of the importance of prayer in the lives of Muslims

● think about the ways in which Muslims believe prayer can bring individuals closer to Allah

● consider ways in which prayer can help to build up and strengthen whole communities.

Salah

Salah is one of the most important of the five basic duties of **Islam** as it requires **Muslims** to focus their hearts and minds completely on **Allah** in prayer five times every day. The way in which Muslims pray and the times at which prayers are said are laid down in the **Qur'an**. Muslims can come closer to Allah by performing salah regularly, correctly and with a full understanding of its significance and meaning.

Muslims believe that the purpose of human creation is to worship Allah. Allah declares in the Qur'an:

'And I created not … mankind except that they worship me.'

Qur'an, **surah** 51: 56

Therefore, Muslims believe that whatever we do we must bear in mind that we are doing it for Allah's sake. Only then can we expect to gain any benefit from the performance of salah.

'Salah is important for a number of reasons:

● it brings men and women closer to Allah

● it keeps human beings away from forbidden activities

Muslims at prayer

● it is designed to control evil desires and passions

● it purifies the heart, develops the mind and comforts the soul

● it is a constant reminder of Allah and His greatness

● it develops discipline and will power

● it shows that Islam is one universal family – the ummah

● it is a means of cleanliness, purity and punctuality

● it develops gratitude, humility and refinement

● it is a sign of total obedience to the will of Allah.

Similarly, the Qur'an teaches that if your salah does not improve the way in which you conduct your life, you must think seriously and find out where you are going wrong.'

Imam Aurangzeb Khan

The times of salah

Salah is performed five times every day at special times:

1 Salat-ul-Fajr – between first light and sunrise

2 Salat-ul-Zuhr – just after the sun has left its highest point in the sky

3 Salat-ul-Asr – between mid-afternoon and sunset

4 Salat-ul-Maghrib – between sunset and darkness

5 Salat-ul-Isha – between darkness and dawn.

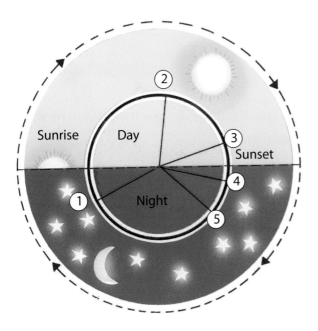

Learning about religion

1 What do you understand by the word 'prayer'? Try to explain it as if to someone who had never heard the word before.

2 Why do you think salah is important in the lives of individual Muslims?

3 **a** Why must the duty to pray at set times during every day present problems for Muslims? Discuss in groups.

b Share your thoughts with another group before sharing with the whole class.

Learning from religion

1 How important do you think salah is for developing Muslims, both as individuals and as a community committed to the worship of Allah?

2 Look carefully at the list of bullet points outlining the importance of salah provided by Aurangzeb Khan.

a Explain how you think salah can fulfil each of these points.

b Place each of Imam Aurangzeb Khan's bullet points into your own rank order of importance. Write them down in order and explain your reasons for the placement of each.

3 Think carefully again about the words of Imam Aurangzeb Khan. In what ways might the world be a better place if everyone were to make time for prayer five times every day? Explain your thoughts carefully.

Worship – Salah 2

In this section you will:

● examine the preparations made by Muslims before they pray

● evaluate the importance of focusing the heart and mind before praying

● find out about the different ways in which Muslims pray.

Preparing for salah

'**Islam** requires **Muslims** to pray five times every day.

'Before we say **salah** we prepare ourselves. In order to focus our hearts and minds on **Allah**, before prayer we wash. This is called **wudu**. Wudu is compulsory and we can not make our salah without first making our wudu.

'Wudu, like salah, is written in the **Qur'an**. It requires the washing of different parts of our bodies, even if we are not very dirty, it is more of a spiritual washing as we prepare to stand before Allah.'

Imam Aurangzeb Khan

After entering into a meditative and prayerful frame of mind by dedicating the wudu that they are about to perform 'In the name of Allah, the most Merciful, the most Kind', Muslims follow a set pattern or ritual:

● the hands are washed up to the wrists three times

● the mouth is rinsed three times

● the nostrils are washed three times as is the tip of the nose

● the face is washed thoroughly three times

● both arms are washed up to the elbow three times

A Muslim performing wudu

● wet hands are then passed over the hair from the forehead to the neck

● wet hands are run over the ears and neck

● both feet are washed up to the ankles.

In addition to the daily salah obligations Muslims can also make their own private and personal prayers at any time. This type of prayer is called **du'a**. Du'a is an opportunity for every Muslim to bring before Allah their own individual concerns, for example, to pray for someone who is ill or in particular need. Du'a also provides the opportunity to meditate on the wonderful gifts Allah has given or to seek the strength of Allah to work hard in their religious duties and to become better people.

Du'a prayer

Therefore, different types of prayer can be included in the performance of du'a. These may include:

- adoration – praising Allah for all the wonderful things He has provided

- intercession – praying for the needs of others

- supplication – asking for the strength to overcome the temptations and pressures of the world and to grow in faith

- confession – saying sorry before Allah for the times when the temptations to sin have been too strong to resist.

Learning about religion

❶ Explain why performing wudu is an essential part of salah.

❷ What do you consider to be the main similarities and differences between salah and du'a?

❸ The prophet Muhammad (pbuh) said that salah of the community was many times more powerful than the du'a of the individual.

   a What do you think the prophet meant by this?

   b Do you agree with him or not? Give reasons.

Learning from religion

❶ Muslims perform wudu before they pray even if they are not physically dirty. Consider other ways wudu cleanse and purify Muslims in readiness for salah besides the physical removal of dirt.

❷ Think about times when you have needed to either focus your mind or prepare yourself for something important.

   a What do you do? Give an example.

   b In what ways might going through a set ritual, such as wudu, help to focus the mind effectively?

❸ Write an example of your own du'a prayer which asks for the strength to cope with a particularly difficult situation.

Worship – Sawm

Sawm

Sawm is the fourth pillar of **Islam**. Sawm means 'fasting' and all adult **Muslims** must fast from dawn to sunset every day of **Ramadan**, the ninth month of the Islamic calendar. In practice this means abstaining from eating, drinking, smoking and sexual relations during the hours of daylight. Travellers and those who are ill during Ramadan can put off not eating and drinking and make up for it later.

Sawm can develop self-control and help people to overcome selfishness, greed and laziness. It is in effect an annual opportunity to refresh and refocus the hearts and minds of Muslims in their worship of **Allah**.

By fasting, Muslims experience for themselves what it is like to have an empty stomach. This develops an empathy for all the poor and hungry people in the world. Fasting teaches Muslims to control the love of comfort, it also helps Muslims to control sexual desires. The **Qur'an** is clear in its teaching that eating, comfort and sex are three things which must be kept under control to behave effectively as Allah's servants:

'O you who believe! Fasting is prescribed for you as it was prescribed for those before you that you may become pious.'

Qur'an, **surah** 2: 183

A Muslim family breaking the fast

Fasting therefore is a sign of a truly obedient Muslim. The following actions, however, will break the fast:

1 deliberate eating or drinking

2 anything entering the body through the nose or mouth; this includes smoking

3 having any sexual relations.

Muslims are expected to make an extra effort to refrain from all immoral actions during the fast. They should not tell lies, break a promise or do anything deceitful.

The importance of sawm

The purpose of fasting is to make a Muslim able to control passions and desires, so that they become a person of good deeds and intentions. Similarly, fasting helps to develop an increased awareness of knowing what it is to go without, even for a little while, and to know hunger.

Learning about religion

❶ Allah revealed the first chapters (or surahs) of the Qur'an to Muhammad (pbuh) during the month of Ramadan. Why then do you think that Muslims believe that this is an appropriate time to fast?

❷ Muhammad (pbuh) taught that although a Muslim may fast at any time, the fast of Ramadan is many times more powerful than any other. Why do you think this is so?

❸ From what you have discovered so far, are your views on the importance of the Ramadan fast the same as your views on the importance of salah prayer? What does this tell you about the priorities of Islam as a religion?

At the end of Ramadan Muslims celebrate with a day of thanksgiving and happiness. The festival of **Id-ul-Fitr** is one of the great occasions for the Muslim community. On this day, Muslims offer special prayers at the **mosque** and thank Allah for all His blessings and mercies.

In addition to the compulsory fasting in Ramadan, Muslims may fast during other times of the year in order to refocus their hearts and minds on Allah.

Learning from religion

❶ With a partner discuss what you consider to be the benefits of fasting. In particular consider what people can gain in terms of their own personal spiritual development. Write down your thoughts.

❷ Ramadan is ultimately about raising awareness and changing attitudes.

   a Spend a whole day being polite, considerate, honest, kind and hardworking, that is to say, the whole day being aware and trying to be 'a person of good deeds and intentions'.

   b Keep an hour-by-hour diary of your experience including the challenges it presents.

❸ If it is appropriate, and with permission, try to experience fasting for yourself. You could try perhaps one morning or afternoon, maybe like Muslims you could attempt to fast during the hours of daylight.

   a Write a number of diary entries explaining how you felt during the time of your fast.

   b What do you consider to be the spiritual benefits that can be achieved through fasting?

The mosque

In this section you will:

● find out about the Muslim place of worship

● think about the variety of ways in which the mosque is used by Muslims

● devise your own plan of a mosque that could serve a local Muslim community.

The importance of the mosque

Muslims believe that **Allah** can be worshipped anywhere. The **prophet Muhammad (pbuh)** said:

'Wherever the hour of prayer overtakes you, you shall perform it. Because the whole earth has been turned into a mosque for me.'

Hadith

However, most Muslim communities will have a special building set aside for worship. These special buildings are called **mosques**. Mosques are important as they provide essential facilities for local people.

The main features of a mosque will include:

● the main prayer hall

● a separate section in which women pray

● a domed ceiling symbolizing the heavens above

● a **minaret**, a tower from which the community is called to prayer five times each day

● a **minbar**, a raised platform

● a **mihrab**, an archway showing the exact direction of Makkah.

In addition all mosques will have a supply of running water and separate rooms for women and men to place their shoes and to perform **wudu**.

Purpose-built mosques will often include offices and a number of rooms used for a variety of community needs, including:

● the mosque school where Muslim children can learn Arabic and more about their faith (the **madrasah**)

● for celebrations and parties

● as courts to hear cases relating to Islamic law.

Prayers are said five times every day at the mosque and are lead by the **imam**. At the main Friday prayers the imam will speak to the congregation from the minbar and give sermons explaining the meaning and importance of the Hadiths – the sayings of the prophet Muhammad (pbuh) or the **surahs** (chapters) of the **Qur'an**.

A mosque in Jeddah, Saudi Arabia

'The mosque is important as a focus of community prayer and learning, but for me not as important as my own family as the heart of my religion. The mosque is used regularly, every day, for people to go and pray to Allah and to learn new things, every day of your life. I have spent time at the mosque madrasah, for seven years, I started when I was four, and finished when I was ten.'

Shamira, aged 13

'The most important prayers at the mosque are the Friday lunchtime prayers. I think Friday is important as it shows Islam is separate from other religions, Judaism has Saturday and Christianity Sunday.'

Mudassir, aged 15

Inside the Niujie mosque, the oldest mosque in Beijing, China

Learning about religion

❶ Mosques, whether purpose-built or converted buildings are usually very beautifully decorated. Why do you think that this is so?

❷ As an architect you have been asked to draw up plans for a brand new purpose-built mosque to serve the local Muslim community.

   a Provide a detailed plan of your proposed mosque.

   b Explain the significance and importance of each part of your design.

   c Say how your proposed mosque will make a major contribution to the life and worship of the local Muslim community.

❸ Why do you think Shamira feels her family community to be as important to her development and growth as a Muslim as the local Mosque?

Learning from religion

❶ Islam clearly teaches that Allah can be worshipped anywhere.

   a Why then do you consider there to be a need for mosques?

   b Do you think it would make a significant difference to the religion of Islam if there were no mosques? Make the case for both sides of the debate before explaining why you have made your own decision.

❷ Muslim children very often attend the madrasah at the local mosque.

   a What do you think they can do and learn at the madrasah that isn't possible at school?

   b Why do you think this is important?

❸ **a** How important do you feel it is for religions to have a special day on which to worship?

   b Do you agree with Mudassir that it is important for different religions to have different special days? Give reasons for your answer.

Holy books – the Qur'an

In this section you will:
- find out about the importance of the **Qur'an** for **Muslims**
- consider ways in which the Qur'an is used by Muslims in worship.

The Qu'ran: the word of Allah

Islam teaches that human beings are the servants of **Allah**. This is seen as a great responsibility and so **Muslims** believe that they need guidance to carry out their duties as Allah's servants. Islam teaches that humans are unable to guide themselves because they have many weaknesses and are frail and short-sighted. Muslims believe only Allah is above all things and that it is He alone who has the power to give guidance that is valid for all times and places. Therefore, He has sent **prophets** and messengers to show humanity the right path in life. In addition to this, He has also given holy books for guidance.

'Allah's favours and blessings are countless. He provides us with all that we need. However, Allah's greatest favour is His guidance contained in the books of revelation. The pure, perfect and most useful knowledge comes only from Allah.'
Imam Aurangzeb Khan

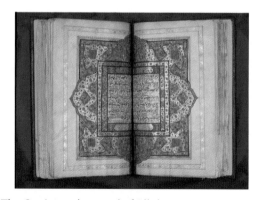

The Qur'an – the word of Allah

The books of Allah

Muslims believe that Allah has inspired all the books which are mentioned in the **Qur'an**. These include the **Tawrah** (Torah) of **Musa** (Moses), the **Zabur** (Psalms) of **Dawud** (David), the **Injil** (Gospel) of **'Isa** (Jesus) and the Qur'an revealed to **Muhammad**. The Qur'an also mentions the **Sahifah of Ibrahim** (Scrolls of Abraham and Moses) (peace be upon them all).

Muslims believe that of all the divine books, only the Qur'an exists in its original, unchanged form. The Zabur, Tawrah and Injil were gradually altered after the death of the prophets to whom they were revealed, and their message changed and distorted. In effect they became a mixture of divine words with those of human beings.

Together all these writings go to make up one divine revelation, although Islam teaches that the Qur'an is most important for guiding human actions. Through these holy writings Allah has shown human beings something of His nature and has told them about the way in which He expects them to live their lives.

The message of the Qu'ran

'The message of the Qur'an is valid for all times and conditions. This is because the Qur'an contains the original messages revealed to Muhammad (**pbuh**). This message, passed from mouth to mouth and from heart to heart for over 1,400 years has enabled Muslims to know the true word of Allah.'

Imam Aurangzeb Khan

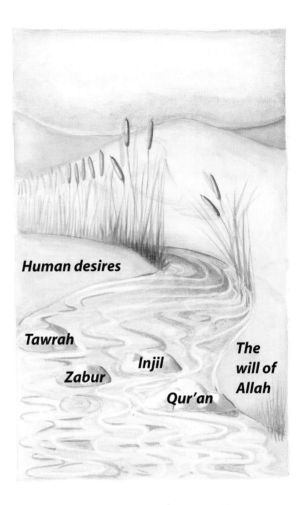

Human desires

Tawrah

Zabur

Injil

Qur'an

The will of Allah

Learning about religion

❶ Explain in your own words what the Qur'an is and why it is so important to Muslims.

❷ Before reading the Qur'an many Muslims will wash their hands, some may choose to take a bath and others, in accordance with the expectations of Islam will perform a complete wudu ritual.

   a What does this tell you about the contents of the Qur'an and its importance for Muslims?

   b In what other ways do you think Muslims might show respect for the Qur'an?

❸ A wealthy Muslim once said, 'Of all riches I love the Qur'an best, take away what you like from me but leave me Allah's words'.

   a How could this man still consider himself rich with just a Qur'an as a possession?

   b Do you agree with him?

Learning from religion

❶ How do you think a book as old as the Qur'an can be of practical use to Muslims today? Can you imagine any lessons that could be for all people for all time?

❷ Look at the picture of 'The way to Allah'. What does this suggest to you about the relationship between the different sources that make up the Qur'an?

❸ Explain why some people hold the view that Jews, Christians and Muslims ought not argue but talk to each other more.

Holy books – Hadiths

In this section you will:

● investigate the ways in which Muslims use the teachings of the prophet Muhammad (pbuh)

● understand the importance of Muhammad (pbuh) as an example to Muslims

● apply the example and teachings of Muhammad (pbuh) to today's world.

The importance of the Hadiths

Hadiths are important to **Muslims**. They are a collection of the words and teachings of the **prophet Muhammad** (**pbuh**) and are used by Muslims as a means of guidance and encouragement in their lives. This means that if ever faced with a difficult decision or dilemma, a Muslim can seek the help of **Allah** through the advice of the prophet Muhammad (pbuh) in the words of the Hadiths.

'No Muslim can underestimate the importance and significance of the Prophet, it was through him that Allah chose to finally reveal Himself both in the words of the Qur'an and in the divine messages revealed though the Hadiths.'

Imam Aurangzeb Khan

Hadiths are used by Muslims to help them live good lives. They provide guidance for living and can be applied to a wide range of social issues and situations.

Examples of Hadiths

1 'The best house among the Muslims is the house in which an orphan is well treated and the worst house among the Muslims is the house in which an orphan is badly treated.'

'One who tries to help the widow and the poor is like a warrior in the way of Allah.'

2 'Guarantee me six things and I shall assure you of paradise. When you speak, speak the truth, keep your promise, discharge your trust, guard your chastity and lower your gaze and withhold your hands from highhandedness.'

'Surely truth leads to virtue, and virtue leads to paradise.'

Muslims discussing the Hadiths

Two 'brother' Muslims

3 'Do not quarrel with your brother Muslim, nor jest with him nor make him a promise which you cannot keep.'

'Each of you is a mirror of his brother, if you see something wrong in your brother, you must tell him to get rid of it.'

'Believers are like the parts of a body to one another each part supporting the others.'

'None of you can be a believer unless he loves for his brother what he loves for himself.'

'A Muslim is he from whose tongue and hands other Muslims are safe.'

4 'Every good action is a charity and it is a good action to meet a friend with a smiling face.'

'There is a man who gives charity and he conceals it so much that his left hand does not know what his right hand spends.'

'Wealth does not come from abundance of goods but from a contented heart.'

5 'The best of you is he who has learnt the Qur'an and then taught it.'

'The seeking of knowledge is a must for every Muslim man and woman.'

'The learned men are the successors of the prophets. They leave behind knowledge as inheritance. One who inherits it obtains a great fortune.'

Learning about religion

❶ Look carefully at the five groups of Hadiths included in this unit.

a What would you say was the moral or religious theme running through each one?

b Why do you think the thoughts and words of Muhammad (pbuh) have been remembered and cherished by Muslims?

c Not all Muslims follow the advice of Muhammad (pbuh) given in the Hadiths very closely at all. Why do you think they chose not to? Provide evidence from the Hadiths to support your answer.

d Why do you think that it is often argued that people should follow the advice and example of their religious leaders or prophets all the time? What reasons would you give?

Learning from religion

❶ Select one group of Hadiths.

a Which group have you selected? Explain your decision.

b To what sort of situation or situations do you think these Hadiths could be applied?

c How could these Hadiths help Muslims to decide how to act in that situation?

d Choose the Hadith with which you most strongly agree and say how you think the world would be improved if everyone adhered to it.

Celebrating festivals

In this section you will:

● find out about the great Muslim festivals of Id-ul-Fitr and Id-ul-Adha

● consider the ways in which celebrating these festivals strengthen both personal faith and community spirit

● evaluate the importance of celebrating religious festivals.

Muslim festivals

There are two great **festivals** in **Islam**, **Id-ul-Fitr** which ends the fast of **Ramadan** and **Id-ul-Adha** which occurs during the month of **Hajj**, the time of pilgrimage to **Makkah**. Both are seen as occasions on which to give thanks to **Allah** for all His blessings and kindness.

Both festivals involve worship and care for others. The whole family (**ummah**) of Islam can feel very much together, celebrating these great festivals although separated around the world, enjoying a time with loved ones and sharing this good feeling by supporting all those who are poor or suffering in any way.

The requirements for feast days are simple:

● cleanliness – baths are taken and clean or new clothes worn

● prayer – **Muslims** come together in huge gatherings, to be as one. This is a very powerful example of the ummah – the Muslim community – as one

● thought for one's own family – presents are given, especially to children, special meals are served

● thought for others – **zakah** is collected and sent off, strangers are welcomed to share in hospitality.

After visiting the **mosque** on feast days, **Muslims** often go home by a different route from the one they took coming, in order to create the largest possible opportunity for meeting other Muslims, and spreading joy.

Id-ul-Fitr

Id-ul-Fitr is the celebration of the end of Ramadan, the month of fasting. The festival begins at the sight of the new moon that welcomes the start of the new month. Muslims celebrate by decorating their houses, giving and receiving cards and gifts and by attending special prayers at the mosque.

Zakah for Id-ul-Fitr is a special payment of a set amount, the equivalent of two meals. This should be given to the poor on behalf of each member of the family by every Muslim who is financially able to do this.

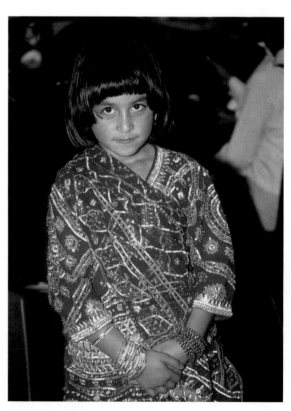

A Muslim dressed for Id

Id-ul-Adha

Id-ul-Adha is important for two reasons. Firstly, it marks the end of the Hajj, the pilgrimage to Makkah. Secondly, it recalls the faith in Allah displayed by the prophet **Ibrahim (pbuh)** when commanded to sacrifice his son **Isma'il** (pbuh).

As with the celebrations of Id-ul-Fitr, cards and gifts are given and received. However, the most important feature of the festival of Id-ul-Adha is the sacrifice of an animal to Allah. The sacrifice recalls the sacrifice of the ram that Allah provided for Ibrahim (pbuh) so he would not have to kill his son Isma'il (pbuh). Muslims may sacrifice sheep, goats, cows and camels. Muslim families enjoy a big meal using the meat from their sacrifice and share the remaining meat with the poor of the community or with friends and relatives.

'I enjoy celebrating Id because it's thanking Allah for the family and friends we have and sharing a happy time with them.'

Shamira, aged 13

Celebrating in the love of Allah

Learning about religion

❶ What do the Id festivals celebrate? In what ways are they similar? In what ways are they different?

❷ Muslims greet each other with shouts of 'Id Mubarak' or 'Happy Id'.

  a What preparations would a Muslim family need to make to ensure a happy Id?

  b How do you think Muslim families/communities in Britain organize the sacrifice and meat distribution? What difficulties might they face? How would these difficulties be overcome?

Learning from religion

❶ In what ways do you think religious festivals like Id-ul-Fitr and Id-ul-Adha bring:

  a communities closer together

  b individuals closer to Allah?

❷ If giving to the poor is so important to Muslims wouldn't it be better not to celebrate such festivals, save the money and give it to the poor? What do you think? Share your thoughts with a partner before writing them down.

In this section you will:

- investigate the reasons for making pilgrimage to Makkah
- understand the nature and importance of entering the state of **ihram**
- develop an awareness of the spiritual transformation that Hajj can have in the lives of Muslim pilgrims.

Pilgrimage to Makkah

Hajj is the fifth pillar of **Islam**. It is a pilgrimage to **Makkah** and is to be made at least once in a lifetime by those **Muslims** who can afford to do so.

When Muslims pray they face the direction of Makkah. In fact they face the **Ka'bah**, the House of Allah, which Muslims believe was built originally by **Adam** (the first man) and later rebuilt by the prophet **Ibrahim** and his son **Isma'il** (peace be upon them all). It was the first house ever built for the sole purpose of the worship of Allah. Muslims believe that Allah has blessed the Ka'bah. Every year, Muslims who can afford to make the journey and are physically fit come here from all over the world to join fellow Muslims in worship in Allah's House.

During Hajj the Islamic community (the **ummah**) becomes particularly evident and can be experienced in a special way by everyone who takes part. Barriers of language, territory, colour and race disappear as the bond of **faith** is strengthened. Everyone has the same status in the House of Allah – the status of His servant.

The Ka'bah

'It was the most amazing moment of my life. Standing before God at the foot of Mount Mercy with 2,000,000 of my fellow Muslims really did bring my faith alive for me. I have always tried hard to keep the teachings of the Qur'an, and live my life as a good person, but this was different. Everything that I have ever been taught, the events in the life of the Prophet that I had only heard about was real. To bear witness with so many others is an experience that I shall never forget.'

Mamood, aged 24 – **Hajji**

Muslims in ihram

Ihram

While approaching Makkah before the Hajj begins, a pilgrim must put on ihram. For men, ihram consists of two sheets of unsewn white cloth. This is a very simple form of dress which male pilgrims must wear in place of their normal everyday clothes. For a woman, ihram does not require special clothes, but they do have to dress simply and wear a veil covering their hair.

This change is very significant. It reminds the pilgrim of his position in relation to Allah. He is a humble servant of his Creator. It also reminds him that after death he will be wrapped in white sheets; not in expensive or fashionable clothes.

There are restrictions on pilgrims while in the state of ihram. He or she must not:

- use perfume
- kill or harm animals, even insects
- break or uproot plants
- do anything dishonest or arrogant
- carry weapons
- cover the head (males)
- cover the face (females)
- wear shoes covering ankles
- cut hair
- clip nails
- have sexual relations.

Learning about religion

1 In your own words define what is meant by 'pilgrimage'.

2 Why do you think Hajj has been included as one of the five pillars of Islam?

3 How essential do you consider ihram to be for Muslim pilgrims to focus their hearts and minds entirely upon Allah?

Learning from religion

1 Do you think going on pilgrimage really makes a difference to the faith of an individual? Give reasons for your answer.

2 Imagine if you were to interview a Muslim about making pilgrimage to Makkah. What reasons do you think they'd give for entering a state of ihram?

3 What benefits would you find going on pilgrimage or a trip, not necessarily to a place of religious significance, but to somewhere special to you? How could such an activity help to focus your heart and mind, and maybe make you a better person?

Pilgrimage – Hajj 2

In this section you will:

- find out about the duties performed by Muslims on Hajj
- discuss the importance of each duty of Hajj
- share your own views on the importance of pilgrimage in Muslim religious life.

The duties of Hajj

Muslims performing **Hajj** and in a state of ihram can truly be described as one equal family before **Allah**. It is as one family that the essential duties or rituals of Hajj are performed.

- The **Ka'bah** is circled seven times. The Ka'bah is thought by Muslims to be the very first place used to worship Allah. Pilgrims run between the hills of **Safa** and **Marwah** where **Hajar**, wife of the prophet **Ibrahim** (**pbuh**), desperately searched for water for her child.

Allah provided water in the form of the Well of Zamzam where pilgrims still stop to drink and to fill bottles to take some of the water home.

- Pilgrims then travel out of Makkah along the plain of **Arafat**. Here around two million pilgrims camp as they perform the next duties of Hajj.

- Pilgrims stand together before Allah on Mount Arafat (The Mount of Mercy). It is an opportunity to commit oneself again to Allah and to follow His laws in all aspects of life.

- The camp then moves on to Muzdalifah, which is between Arafat and Makkah. Here pilgrims collect small stones to throw at the pillars at **Mina**.

- Mina is the where the prophet Ibrahim (pbuh) and his family resisted the temptations of the devil to turn away from Allah and to put their trust in him. Pilgrims throw stones at three stone pillars that represent the devil. This symbolizes a rejection of both the devil that tempted Ibrahim (pbuh) and also at the 'devil' inside that leads everyone into temptation.

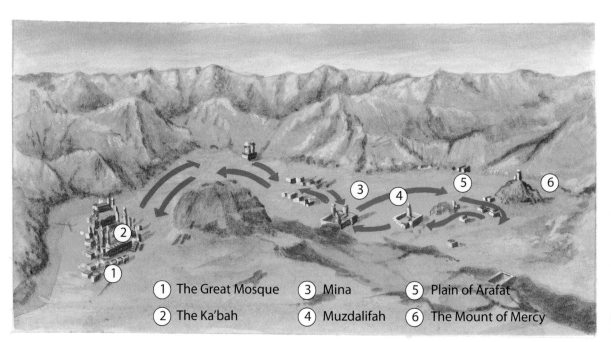

①	The Great Mosque	③	Mina	⑤	Plain of Arafat
②	The Ka'bah	④	Muzdalifah	⑥	The Mount of Mercy

The route of the Hajj

- The pilgrims then camp at Mina for two days to celebrate the Feast of Sacrifice (**Id-ul-Adha**). An animal is sacrificed in thanksgiving for the ram Allah gave Ibrahim (pbuh), just as Ibrahim (pbuh) was about to sacrifice his son **Isma'il** (pbuh) to Allah.

- As an outward sign of the completion of the duties of Hajj men will have their heads shaved (unfurling) and women at least 2.5cm cut from their hair.

- Pilgrims will then return to Makkah to circle the Ka'bah again before returning to their homes.

Male Muslims who have performed Hajj are entitled to take the name **Hajji** and women **Hajjah**.

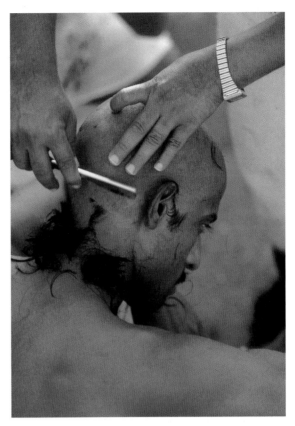

The unfurling

Learning about religion

❶ Many Muslims spend a long time saving up and planning for the Hajj pilgrimage. Usually a little help is appreciated! Working in small groups and using the information available to you, devise a travel brochure that will outline everything a pilgrim needs to know before going on Hajj. Be sure to include information for pilgrims concerning:

- travel arrangements
- itinerary
- specific needs as Muslim travellers.

❷ Using each duty of Hajj as a subtitle:

a evaluate the difference experiencing each one can make in the lives of pilgrims

b choose one or two duties that you consider to be of greatest importance for Muslim pilgrims. Explain why they are important and why you have chosen them.

Learning from religion

❶ Those who have completed Hajj are honoured by the names Hajji (male) and Hajjah (female). What difference could people so honoured make to the life of their local ummah or community, especially among those who have never been on Hajj?

❷ 'Pilgrimage is costly and old fashioned, you're better off staying home. This is where religion really matters.'

a Why would someone make this claim?

b Do you agree or disagree with this point of view? What reasons would you give for your view?

Rites of passage

In this section you will:

● discover the ways in which Muslims celebrate birth

● understand the importance of marriage in the Muslim community

● express reasons why the marking of such occasions is an important part of the life of individuals and communities.

Everyone enjoys a celebration. Finding an excuse for a party or sharing a good time with family and friends is not difficult. However, the reasons behind some celebrations are very important – the birth of a baby or the joining together of two people in marriage are important to both religious and non-religious people alike. This is an opportunity to discover something of the way in which **Muslims** mark these two special occasions, referred to as rites of passage, in a special way.

Birth

For Muslims, the birth of a baby is a reason for great joy. Muslims believe that **Allah** has granted the family the blessing of a son or daughter and so should receive their thanks and praise.

A new born baby hearing the adhan for the first time

The new baby is welcomed into the community of **Islam** as soon as it is born, as the head of the family whispers the **adhan** (the call to prayer) into its ear. Therefore, the first word the baby hears is 'Allah'. Prayers, usually led by the community's imam, are said for the baby and the family.

Marriage

Muhammad (**pbuh**) said:

'A woman should only be married to a person who is good enough for her or compatible to her.'
Hadith

For Muslims, the only sort of compatibility that really matters is **faith**. Muhammad (pbuh) permitted marriages between people of vastly different social status and financial backgrounds, knowing that compatibility depended more on what they were like in their hearts and in their devotion to Allah.

The most important ingredients in a Muslim marriage are shared values and **beliefs**, so that even if the couple come from different cultures and backgrounds, they will possess the same basic religious attitudes and practices which will help to bind them ever closer together.

'Do not marry only for a person's looks, their beauty might become the cause of moral decline.'

'Do not marry for wealth, since this may become the cause of disobedience. Marry rather on the grounds of religious devotion.'

Hadiths

Islam regards marriage as the normal duty of every human being. Finding a good life partner, and building up a relationship together is regarded as an essential part of the faith.

A Muslim marriage

The Muslim marriage service is a social ceremony rather than a religious one and so can take place anywhere licensed for marriages. However, prayers seeking Allah's blessing led by the imam, will be said for the couple and their families.

In the Muslim world, there is often little contact between young men and women. The selection of a marriage partner is often made by the parents. Sometimes they will look for a known member of the family, preferably a cousin. For many couples, love is expected to come after the marriage and not before.

It is true to say that today, in some Muslim families, customs are changing a little with regards to the selection of marriage partners. Although there is still an expectation that partners will be suitable for each other in the eyes of their families, some couples are happier considering for themselves their own suitability for each other.

'The best of treasures is a good wife. She is pleasing in her husband's eyes, looks for ways to please him, and takes care of his possessions while he is away, the best of you are those who treat their wives best.'

Hadith

Learning about religion

❶ Why is it important that a Muslim child should hear the adhan as soon as it is born?

❷ What does this suggest to you about the relationship between the child and Allah?

❸ Explain why marriage is important to Muslims. If marriage is so important to the growth and development of Muslim communities, why do you think it is treated as a secular rather than a religious occasion?

Learning from religion

❶ Why do you think people consider the marking of rites of passage as important?

❷ The prophet Muhammad (pbuh) said, 'Whoever gets married has completed half of his faith; therefore let him be conscious of Allah in the other half of his faith.'

   a   What do you think the prophet meant by this?

   b   Do you consider that a Muslim's first duty is towards Allah or towards the family? Or are they really both the same? Explain your answers.

❸ What are the strengths and weaknesses of arranged marriages? Should parents decide on their children's marriage partners, or should it be left entirely to those contemplating marriage? Show that you have considered more than one point of view before giving a final answer.

Creation

In this section you will:

- find out about Muslim beliefs regarding the creation of the universe
- compare and contrast the Muslim beliefs about creation with those of Jews and Christians
- discuss the importance of the Islamic understanding of creation for Muslims today.

The power of Allah

Most religious traditions have developed an account of **creation** that depicts the central involvement of God. The **Qur'an** is very clear as to the origins of all things, all things derive their being from **Allah** and to Allah shall all return when their time on earth is over.

'It is Allah who has created the heavens and the earth, and all that is between them in six days. Then he rose to His throne that suits His majesty. Mankind has no God besides Allah, as protector and helper. Remember this, Allah manages and regulates every thing on earth and in heaven and when every thing has had its time it will return to Him.'

'Allah alone is the all-knower of the seen and unseen, the all-mighty, the most merciful. It was He who created all goodness and began the creation of Mankind from clay. Then He made offspring – male and female. Then He made all other living things upon earth.'

Qur'an, from surahs 21 and 32

At the completion of His creation Allah declared:

'Have they not looked at the heaven above them, how We have made it and adorned it, and there are no rifts in it?

Earth from space

And the earth! We have spread it out, and set thereon mountains standing firm, and have produced therein every kind of lovely growth in pairs.'

Qur'an, **surah** 50: 6–7

The creation

Muslims have a very clear understanding of how the whole universe came about: it was created by Allah. The Qur'an teaches that all things were summoned into existence at Allah's command in pairs so that creation may be seen as a perfectly balanced order. Such a balance can be understood in the creation of the sky and the earth, the sea and dry land, light and darkness and male and female.

In common with the Jewish Torah and Christian Bible the Qur'an tells of creation covering six days. However, Muslims are certain that if Allah had wished, He could have created everything in just 'a twinkling of the eye'.

Similarly, the Qur'an mentions the creation of beings for whom creation is not mentioned in either the Torah or Bible.

For example, Muslims believe in common with Jews and Christians that human beings were created from clay, they also believe that **angels** (slaves of Allah who always do His will) were created from light and that **jinn** (beings created with free will, living on earth in a separate yet parallel world to our own) were created from fire. However, of all of Allah's creations, this planet and in particular the human beings that inhabit it are the most important.

A famous story illustrates the importance of the creation of humans. After the creation of **Adam** (**pbuh**), the first man, Allah brought all the angels and all the jinn before Adam (pbuh) and commanded them to bow down to him as he was the most wonderful thing that Allah had ever created. All the angels and jinn bowed down with the exception of one jinn called **Shaytan** (the Devil). As a punishment Allah banished Shaytan from His presence and in return Shaytan vowed to spend all his time and power tempting humans to go against the will of Allah and to sin.

Learning about religion

❶ Explain why a Muslim could never accept that:

   a   the universe came into being by chance

   b   there was no evidence for the existence of Allah.

❷ Read carefully the quotation from Qur'an, surah 50: 6–7.

   a   Explain in your own words what it teaches about creation as the work of Allah

   b   Why do you think that it is important that everything is created in pairs?

❸ '(False gods) cannot create a fly … nor could they ever snatch back what a fly might snatch from them.' (Qur'an, surah 22: 73). What evidence is there to suggest that Muslims believe that Allah is the one true God?

Learning from religion

❶ Using a Bible, look up the Book of Genesis and read Chapter 1 to Chaper 2, verse 4a. These verses detail the Jewish and Christian accounts of creation.

   a   What are the similarities between this account and Muslim beliefs about creation?

   b   Are there any major differences? Write down your findings.

❷ Some people have criticized all three accounts and said that they are not accurate, that they are myths.

   a   With a partner discuss what is meant by 'myth'.

   b   What important truths do you think these creation myths convey to Muslims, Christians and Jews?

❸ Shaytan vowed to tempt humanity away from Allah.

   a   What evidence might people present to convince others that Shaytan actually does this?

   b   What other ways might there be of understanding this same evidence?

Environment

In this section you will:

● understand the Muslim belief that all creation is Allah's

● discuss the ways in which Allah has placed humans on earth to act as His stewards

● evaluate the claim that humans do not always live up to the responsibilities Allah has given them.

A tropical rain forest

Allah's gift of creation

Muslims believe that **Allah** has given this planet to humankind to look after and protect. The **Qur'an** teaches that human beings have been created by Allah and placed on earth to act as stewards (**khalifah**) and take responsibility for every part of Allah's creation. They are expected not to pollute or damage the world. Instead they are expected to protect the fine balance that makes up Allah's creation. As a result, Muslims are commanded to make careful use of resources like water, respect animals and replace natural resources used wherever possible.

'It is He who has made you custodians, inheritors of the Earth.'

Qur'an, **surah** 6: 165

Care for all creatures

Muslims can expect to be judged by Allah on their stewardship of His creation, including all creatures and all the natural resources which He has given.

Many Muslims are concerned with the well being of the other creatures, besides human beings that Allah has placed on the planet. It is true that some animals have been given by Allah as food but **Muhammad** (**pbuh**) banned any 'sport' which involved making animals fight each other, which was common in his time. Therefore, modern blood sports such as fox-hunting are condemned by Islam.

Islam teaches that no one should ever hunt just for amusement. Muslims believe that people should only take the life of animals for food or another useful purpose.

Respecting all that Allah has created

'If someone kills a sparrow for sport, the sparrow will cry out on the Day of Judgement, "O Lord! That person killed me for nothing! He did not kill me for any useful purpose!"'

Hadith

All hunting should be for food, and any animal used for hunting should be well trained and kept under control.

Experiments are carried out on animals for a variety of reasons. Some of these are medical others are for cosmetic purposes. According to the principle of compassion and kindness towards all Allah's creations, any experiment simply for the development of luxury goods is forbidden. Muslims should always find out if the things they buy have been produced using **halal** (permitted by Allah) methods.

With regard to medical experiments, if there were no possible alternative to an experiment on an animal, then Muslims might accept it. However, they would prefer to look for some other method of investigation.

'Allah it is He who has subjected … to you all that is in the Heavens and all that is in the Earth.'

Qur'an, surah 45: 12–13

Human responsibility

Muslims believe that Allah has given people free will and it is as free agents that we decide how we treat the planet we live on. However, Islam teaches that this planet is a place created out of love, and therefore it should be looked after through love.

Islam teaches that Muslims should seek to live at peace with nature, and to bring about a oneness between human beings and the rest of Allah's creation.

Learning about religion

❶ Why do you think Allah has made humans khalifah? Why not look after the planet himself?

❷ How do Muslims use passages revealed to Muhammad (pbuh) in the Qur'an to support their opinion?

❸ Does this view hold any implications for the way in which human beings should treat this planet?

Learning from religion

❶ a Think of five different ways in which human beings act as khalifah.

b Are there also ways in which animals and plants also seem to work to protect the environment?

❷ What evidence is there to support the claim that human beings have not always proved to be very good khalifah? What can be done to improve things?

❸ Is there anything you could do? For example, on a very simple level you could always put litter in bins or switch off unnecessary lights. Think about it, write it down and go and do it!

Abuses of Allah's creation

In this section you will:

- develop an understanding of creation as Allah's gift to humanity
- consider ways in which people abuse Allah's gift
- develop your thinking on ways in which humans can work to be better stewards of Allah's creation.

The **Qur'an** teaches that we have been placed on earth to act as stewards (**khalifah**). This means to look after **Allah**'s creation on His behalf. Sadly, there is a good deal of evidence to suggest that we do not always do a very satisfactory job. Many people abuse Allah's created order by a misuse of nature and worse still by abusing the greatest of all Allah's creation, themselves.

The planet

Abuse of Allah's creation goes on all around the world. One of the main concerns is the ways in which the vast tropical rain forests are being cut down at a very fast rate. It may well be the case that the timber cut is required for building projects, or the land cleared needed to graze herds of cattle, but the rain forests have been provided by Allah for a particular reason. Carbon dioxide, produced when something is burned, is turned into oxygen by trees. The more trees the more oxygen, but fewer trees means more carbon dioxide in the atmosphere.

Ourselves

Another concern held by **Muslims** is the way in which people abuse themselves by the use of alcohol. The use of all alcohol is strictly

Destroying the rain forest

Muhammad spoke out against the use of alcohol

forbidden in **Islam**. This applies not only to wine which existed at the time of **Muhammad (pbuh)** but also to any other form of alcohol. The main reason for this is that alcohol can cause people to lose control over their own minds and bodies. A famous story told by Muslims illustrates this fact well.

'Intoxicants are the key to all evils. A man was brought and asked either to tear the Holy Qur'an, or kill a child, or bow in worship to an idol, or drink alcohol, or sleep with a woman. He thought the less sinful thing was to drink the alcohol, so he drank it. Then he slept with the woman, killed the child, tore the Holy Qur'an and bowed in worship of the idol.'

A Muslim tale

Islam teaches that **Shaytan** uses different ways to turn people away from belief in Allah, and alcohol is just one.

At the time of Muhammad (pbuh), many people enjoyed drinking alcohol. The teaching of Allah in the Qur'an took human weakness into account, and the prohibition of alcohol was given in stages.

As the news of this latest revelation spread through Madinah, the city in which Muhammad (pbuh) was living, the effect was amazing. People poured away the drinks they held in their hands, and smashed their wine containers, pouring the liquid away. Few, if any, true Muslims have ever touched alcohol since.

Learning about religion

❶ 'Alcohol is a pleasant social habit, the best expression of hospitality.' Why would a Muslim disagree with this statement?

❷ What are your views on the use of alcohol? Do you agree with the teachings of Islam? Support your answers with reasons and examples.

❸ 'I know that smoking is bad for you, but it's my life and I'll do what I like with it!'

   a How would a Muslim respond to this statement?

   b What reasons would they give for their opinions?

Learning from religion

❶ In what sense can it be said that the world is Allah's gift to humanity?

❷ Imagine that someone has given you a very precious gift and hopes you'd look after it – rather like the gift of creation that Allah has given to us.

   a Discuss with a partner how that person would feel if you treated their gift disrespectfully and damaged it.

   b Use the results of your discussions to write down how Allah must view our abuse of the beautiful gift He has given us.

❸ What can be done to safeguard the environment so that it can be passed on to future generations in good shape?

Human rights

In this section you will:

● discover what is meant by 'human rights'

● understand the importance of basic human rights for Muslims.

Human rights and responsibilities

Islam teaches that all human beings have been created by **Allah**. As a result **Muslims** believe that there are basic rights which are shared by all people and which should be observed in every society, whether the society is Islamic or not.

These human rights have been granted by Allah, and not by any ruler or government, and it is the duty of Muslims to protect them actively. Failure to do so can lead to people being oppressed and living life in misery. Muslims believe that human life is sacred, and that all human beings should be treated with respect.

The earth has many wonderful resources, and there is enough for everyone to live well. No human being should know hunger while others are able to waste what they have. Islam teaches that the needs of the suffering must be met. The hungry should be fed, the naked clothed, and the wounded or diseased given medical treatment, whether they are Muslim or not, and whether they are friends or enemies.

The ummah before Allah

Sufferers of famine

Muslims also believe that the honour and dignity of every individual is important. Therefore, ridicule is never seen as fun, especially when there is arrogance or malice behind it. Muslims believe that we may laugh with people, to share in the happiness of life but we must never laugh at people which may cause them distress or embarrassment.

Muslims believe that no attempt should ever be made to force people to act against their own will, so long as they are not acting against the best interests of others.

Muslims believe that no human being should ever be imprisoned unless they are proved guilty of some crime, in an open and unbiased court.

Muslims believe that the power of any human being is only given on trust from Allah. It is therefore their duty to speak out against dictators, and protect the weak from those who would oppress them. To Muslims, a dictator is a ruler who attempts to assert his own will upon the people, rather than seek for them the will of Allah which is always based on kindness and justice.

Learning about religion

❶ From a Muslim point of view what do you understand by the term 'human rights'?

❷ Explain fully why honouring basic human rights is so important in Islam.

❸ Using the information available to you in this chapter:

   a select one basic right that Muslims would agree has been granted by Allah to all people

   b write a short statement outlining your reasons for your choice

   c list two or three examples of this right being denied people

   d what do you think could or should be done in this these situations?

Learning from religion

❶ Today most people would want to claim their basic human rights as one of their most treasured possessions.

   a Think about a possession of which you are particularly fond. Describe what it is and explain how and why you treat it differently from your other possessions.

   b In what ways can this possession be said to be valuable to you?

❷ What things can be said to be valuable but worth very little money? List some.

❸ From your understanding of Muslim views regarding human rights, explain why it is true that Allah has given us many valuable things which are worth very little in a financial sense. Illustrate your answers with examples.

Caring for others – Zakah

In this section you will:

● investigate zakah, the third pillar of Islam

● consider ways in which zakah can make a difference in the lives of all Muslims

● evaluate the significant contribution such a system could make if adopted by all.

A Muslim making a zakah contribution

Caring for others

All **Muslims** are expected to be charitable in hospitality and in caring for the wider community. For example a baker's shop could give away what it had left on a Thursday night, so that no one nearby need say their Friday prayers hungry. Similarly, a Muslim could send money to support an appeal or disaster fund.

The **prophet Muhammad** (**pbuh**) encouraged giving:

'He who eats and drinks while his brother goes hungry, is not one of us.'

Hadith

'Every day two **angels** come down from Heaven; one of them says "O **Allah**! Compensate every person who gives in Your name.' The other says "O Allah! Destroy every miser!"'

Hadith

Zakah

In addition to such charitable giving, Muslims are expected to share their income and wealth as a matter of duty, and to hand over a certain proportion each year to support those who are less fortunate in the community. This is not regarded as a matter of choice, but as a religious duty and is called **zakah**.

Zakah is the third pillar of **Islam**. The Arabic word 'zakah' means 'to purify or cleanse'. Zakah is to be paid once a year on savings at the rate of two-and-a-half percent. Payment of zakah is a means of keeping wealth clear of greed and selfishness. It also encourages Muslims to be honest.

Zakah is a compulsory payment and is not seen by Muslims as a charity or a tax. Charity is optional and taxes can be used by the state for any purpose, but zakah has to be spent for purposes like helping the poor, the needy,

Helping the poor

Rates of zakah

Wealth	Amount	Rate
Cash in hand or bank	Over the value of 595g of silver	2.5%
Gold and silver	85g of gold or 595g of silver	2.5%
Trading goods	To the value of 595g of silver	2.5%
Cows	30	1
Goats and sheep	40	1
Mining produce	Any	20%

Agricultural produce	Per harvest:
	    Rain watered land
	    Irrigated
		
		10%
		5%

payment of salaries to its collectors, to free captives and debtors, and for travellers in need. Zakah is an act of worship and obedience. Muslims pay zakah to gain Allah's favour. Zakah provides Muslims with the opportunity of sharing wealth with those less fortunate.

Muslims see wealth as really belonging to Allah. He is seen as the real owner and people are merely the trustees of His wealth. Through the payment of zakah, the rich share their wealth with the poor and thus a fair distribution of resources is ensured.

Learning about religion

❶ What is zakah, and why do you think that it has been included as one of the five essential religious duties of all Muslims?

❷ Using the information available explain why zakah is not just another form of taxation. How is it different?

❸ Zakah means 'to purify or cleanse'. How can paying zakah be said to purify or cleanse those who pay it?

Learning from religion

❶ In the Qur'an it is written: 'And whoever is mean, it is only at the expense of his own soul.' (Qur'an, surah 47: 38). What are the implications of this verse for:

a   individual Muslims

b   a local Muslim community

c   the whole world?

❷ 'Showing care and love for other people is exactly the same as showing care and love for Allah.' Why is this true? Give reasons.

❸ Islam teaches that caring for others goes far beyond giving a certain amount of goods and money each year. Time and effort given over to assisting others is equally important. Find out something of the work of the Islamic organization the Red Crescent, as it tries to bring relief and comfort to those in greatest need.

Women in Islam

In this section you will:

● find out about what the Qur'an teaches regarding the status of women in Islam

● investigate issues relating to modern Muslim women

● evaluate the claim that Islam is fair to both women and men.

Women have a very important place in **Islamic** society. The importance of women as mothers and as wives was made clear by **Muhammad (pbuh)**:

'Paradise lies at the feet of your mothers.'

Once a person asked Muhammad (pbuh), 'Who deserves the best care from me?' The prophet replied, 'Your mother, then your mother then your mother then your father and then your nearest relatives.'

'O people, your wives have certain rights over you and you have certain rights over them.'

The prophet also said:

'The best amongst you is the one who is best towards his wife.'

Hadiths

These sayings indicate the important position that should be granted to women in Islam. However, there are some people who have misgivings about the status of women in Islam. For some, a **Muslim** woman is seen almost as a prisoner in the four walls of her own house, a non-person, someone who has no rights and is living under the domination of men.

A group of Muslim women

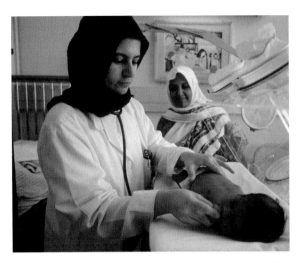

A Muslim woman at work

Muslims believe that **Allah** has created all living creatures in pairs, male and female, including humankind. Allah has honoured the children of **Adam** (pbuh) both male and female. As a result, Muslim women have certain rights and responsibilities, for example, the right to choose their husband. No one can impose a decision on a woman against her will. She has a right to seek separation from her husband if their marriage becomes impossible to sustain.

A woman has a right to develop her talents and to work. Islam allows a non-Muslim married woman to keep and practise her religion and her husband cannot interfere with this freedom. This would apply for example to Christian and Jewish women with Muslim husbands.

It is the duty of the Muslim mother to bring up children according to the **faith** of Islam, to look after the family and control domestic affairs. Muslim women should dress modestly, as should Muslim men. In some Muslim countries, Women put on **hijab** (a covering cloak) while going out and meeting adult males other than close relatives.

Islam views a husband and wife as complementary to each other. Neither should dominate the other. Each has his or her own individual rights and duties and together they should form a peaceful and happy family, which Islam teaches is the basis for a sound and prosperous society.

Learning about religion

❶ The prophet Muhammad (pbuh) particularly emphasized the importance of the role of the mother in the Muslim family. Why do you think he did so?

❷ The Qur'an states that Allah has created everything 'in pairs'.

   a How is this apparent in Muslim family life?

   b This suggests that women and men are both equally important in the sight of Allah but do not have identical roles. Explain why this is the case and what you feel about it.

Learning from religion

❶ Traditionally, Islam has taught that women, although equal to men before Allah, should be obedient to their husbands.

   a How can such teaching strengthen marriages?

   b Can you think of times when Muslim women ought not to be obedient to their husbands? Give examples of such occasions.

❷ How complicated do you think it would be to bring up children born into a mixed marriage? (For example a Christian or Jewish wife married to a Muslim husband.) What do you think would be required of all involved to ensure success and happiness?

Matters of life and death

In this section you will:

● understand what is meant by the term 'human life is sacred'

● consider Islamic teaching regarding the afterlife

● apply Islamic teaching to issues surrounding abortion and euthanasia.

Muslims believe that all human life is a gift of **Allah**, and is therefore sacred.

'Do not kill anyone … killing Allah has forbidden.'
Qur'an, surah 17: 33

'It is He, Allah, Who makes laugh, and makes weep. It is Allah Who causes death and gives life. And that He Allah creates the pairs, male and female.'
Qur'an, surah 53: 42–5

Muslims believe that Allah has given every life an allotted span. No human being knows when their life will be required by Allah and taken back. Therefore, it is the duty of all Muslims to live every day as if it was their last in readiness for the moment when they will face Allah and answer to Him for what they have done with their lives.

'The knowledge of the Final Hour is with Allah; none can reveal the time but He. It shall not come upon you except all of a sudden.'
Qur'an, surah 7: 187

Islam teaches that death itself should never be feared. It is human nature to dread pain and suffering, but Muslims should do their best to bear everything with patience and fortitude. Death is the natural end of human life. It cannot be avoided, and no one escapes it.

'When their time comes, neither can they delay nor can they advance it an hour.'
Qur'an, surah 16: 61

Muslims should not fear death, nor consider it to be the end of everything, as they believe in the promise of an afterlife. This should be a time of great joy and reward for all their efforts on earth.

In effect human life is one eternal life made up of two parts, life before and life after death. Muslims believe that the spirit of life that Allah has breathed into everyone is raised by Allah, from death to the afterlife.

'Do you think that We shall not reassemble your bones? Yes, We are able to put together in perfect order the tips of fingers!'
Qur'an, surah 75: 3

Islam, therefore, teaches that death is beyond human control. No person can choose the time of their passing – it is Allah alone who sanctions the hour of death.

'No person can die except by Allah's leave and after an appointed term.'
Qur'an, surah 3: 145

A Muslim tombstone

Islam teaches that funerals should not be expensive. Muslims prefer that coffins should not be used, except to comply with local regulations for health reasons. Ideally, the body should be buried simply in the earth, and should be carried to the cemetery.

Muslims are usually buried with their face turned to the right, facing **Makkah**. It is therefore preferable if they can have their own cemeteries, or their own special plot so that they may have their graves facing in the right direction.

As the body is lowered, they say:

'In the name of God we commit you to the earth, according to the Way of the **Prophet** of God.'

A little earth is then thrown down with the words:

'We created you from it, and We return you into it, and from it We will raise you a second time.'

Qur'an, surah 20: 55

Money should not be spent on elaborate tombstones or memorials, but donations given to the poor.

Mourning should not last for more than three days, except for widows who may mourn for four months and ten days, and should not remarry during that period.

Learning from religion

❶ Think about the word 'sacred'. What does it mean?

❷ What do you think Muslims mean when they say human life is sacred? In what ways does the Muslim funeral practice confirm that human life is sacred?

❸ Why can death been seen as a time of hope as well as sadness for Muslims?

Learning about religion

❶ Should the fact that human life is sacred make a difference to the way in which we treat other people?

❷ Working with a partner, discuss the following moral dilemmas from a Muslim point of view. Compare these with your own views and your reasons for holding them.

a An unmarried woman falls pregnant and is uncertain about how she feels. She is faced with a number of possibilities:

● to have the baby and bring it up

● to have the baby and put it up for adoption

● to have an abortion.

What advice would you give her? Upon what evidence would you base your advice? Explain why you would reject certain options.

b A 63-year-old grandfather, is diagnosed as suffering from an incurable form of cancer. He has been told that he will die soon and will suffer a lot of pain. He asks a doctor to end his life painlessly with a lethal injection before the cancer takes a complete hold on his body. The request is denied as euthanasia is against the law in Britain.

Do you think Muslims would support the man's request or do you think that they would agree with the law on euthanasia as it stands? What alternatives might the Muslim community suggest? What might be their motives for such suggestions?

Jihad

In this section you will:
- investigate the nature of **jihad** in Islam
- examine the reasons for the inclusion of jihad in the Muslim life of faith
- consider the strengths and weaknesses of jihad in modern society.

The nature of jihad

Jihad is an Arabic word that means 'striving'. **Muslims** use the word jihad to refer to any activity undertaken for the love of **Allah**. Jihad is the use of all one's energies and resources to establish the **Islamic** way of life. Jihad is, therefore, a continuous process for Muslims.

'The aim of jihad is to establish peace. At first we learn to control bad desires and intentions. Human beings must strive hard to achieve this. This is jihad within ourselves and is the basis for the jihad which is concerned with establishing right and removing evil from lives and from society, to establish peace.'

Imam Aurangzeb Khan

Therefore, jihad demands the use of all material and mental resources. It may be the case that Muslims may be required to give their lives for the cause of Islam.

The aim of jihad is to seek the pleasure of Allah. This must not be forgotten because this purpose is the basis of all Islamic practice. Jihad fits alongside the basic duties of **shahadah**, **salah**, **zakah**, **sawm** and **hajj**. All these duties teach obedience to Allah and seek His favour so that Muslims may reap the reward of entering Paradise, the place of joy and peace, when they die.

Muslim soldiers

All Islamic duties should prepare Muslims to engage in jihad. Jihad is at the heart of faith and the end result of salah, zakah, sawm and Hajj.

'It is most important that we try hard to practise what we say.'

Imam Aurangzeb Khan

'Why do you ask of others the right conduct and you yourselves forget, have you no sense?'

Qur'an, surah 2: 44

The importance of jihad

'O you who believe! Why do you say that which you do not do? It is most hateful to Allah that you say that which you do not.'

Qur'an, surah 61: 2–3

These verses clearly direct Muslims to put words into action. To achieve this, Muslims carry out their duty to do good themselves and urge others to do the same. This can, and often does, include getting involved in charity and relief organizations like the Red Crescent (the Islamic version of the Red Cross).

However, jihad can also result in a violent struggle in order to establish the Islamic way of life. Such an outcome is tragic as Islam teaches that violence is prohibited unless absolutely necessary. Wherever possible, jihad is centred around changing hearts and minds by peaceful persuasion rather than by force.

A Red Crescent refugee camp

Learning about religion

❶ What is meant by 'jihad'?

❷ Why do you think jihad is considered to be an important feature of Islam?

❸ Jihad has not been included as a 'pillar' of Islam.

   a Why do you think this is so?

   b Look at the pictures on these pages. Explain how jihad can be a path that leads to both violence and peace.

Learning from religion

❶ Islam teaches that unnecessary violence is wrong. However, there are times when most societies find it necessary to fight.

   a Do you think that jihad could ever provide Muslims with a reason to use violence or make war? Provide some examples to support your answers.

   b Do you feel that jihad – 'striving for the cause of Allah' – is likely to be understood and well received by non-Muslims?

   c In what ways could jihad benefit the whole community, both Muslim and non-Muslim?

Evil and suffering

In this section you will:

- think about what is meant by the problem of evil
- consider Muslim responses to the claim that blame for evil and suffering in the world should be laid before Allah
- devise your own arguments to explain the problem of evil.

Everyday the media brings us headlines about things many would describe as 'evil', or about great 'suffering'.

Young family dies in house fire

Man convicted of murder

Earthquake kills thousands

Famine threatens Ethiopia

Leukaemia sufferer, 14, emergency bone marrow transplant essential

The effects of an earthquake

The problem of evil and suffering

Everyday people ask the question 'why?' Why, if there is an almighty God who has created all things out of love and compassion are we to suffer? Is it not impossible to believe in something all-powerful and all-loving that allows evil and suffering to exist? It would seem that either God is not all-powerful or else not all-loving, as evil and suffering clearly exist.

'I look at the sun, moon, sky, lakes and wonderful things like that that Allah can do. Then I look beyond these things, the wonderful things, and I see flooding, hurricanes and droughts. I ask myself, "How can Allah allow such things?"'

Anish, aged 13

Muslim responses

Muslims believe that **Allah** is indeed all-powerful and all-loving and for that reason has granted to all created things free will. It is the murderer who freely decides to take a life and the free and natural course of things for earthquakes to occur.

Muslims believe that the will of Allah is beyond human understanding and therefore impossible to rationalize. Muslims in their prayers will often add 'If Allah wills' as they know that all things beyond our control are in Allah's hands and that they should trust His judgement.

'Or do you think that you shall enter Paradise without such trials as came to those who passed away before you?'

Qur'an, surah 2: 214

'Revile not destiny, for, behold, I am Destiny.'

Hadith

Learning about religion

❶ There are clearly different types of evil and suffering. For example:

- natural evil (including natural disasters)

- moral evil (including the evil humans inflict upon each other).

Look at the examples of evil and suffering included in this unit:

  a divide your page into two

  b head one column 'Natural Evil' and the other 'Moral Evil'

  c write examples of evil and suffering under the headings

  d write a couple of lines to explain your choices

  e in what ways could Allah be to blame in these examples?

What responses do you think a Muslim would make to this question?

Learning from religion

❶ Attempts to vindicate God from blame regarding evil and suffering are called theodicies. Muslims point to free will as the most significant theodicy.

  a Why do you think that this is so?

  b Do you think human beings and the forces of nature enjoy free will?

  c Is this theodicy successful?

❷ Look at the quotations from the Qur'an in this unit. Use them to devise your own theodicy.

The existence of Allah

In this section you will:

● understand the Muslim assertion that the statement 'Allah exists' is a statement of fact

● investigate traditional arguments that have been put forward to demonstrate Allah's existence

● consider the validity of such arguments and to put forward alternative views.

Moved by the power of Allah

Faith and trust

To be a true **Muslim** one must be able to proclaim the **faith** of the **shahadah**:

'Ash hadu an laa ilaha il-allahu wa Ash hada anna Muhammadar abduhu wa rasulu.'

(I believe there is no god but Allah; and I believe that Muhammad is the servant and messenger of Allah.)

For a Muslim to state 'I believe' indicates an acceptance of the reality of **Allah** in their hearts and minds.

'For all who profess the shahadah, Allah is as real as the beating of their own heart, He is the creator and sustainer of all things, there is no doubt of Allah's presence in the universe, no need to prove He exists.'

Imam Aurangzeb Khan

Arguments for the existence of Allah

For some people who are not Muslims the concept and existence of Allah can be difficult to understand and accept. For this reason Muslim scholars developed an argument to prove to all people that Allah must exist.

The 'Kalam argument' contends that:

● all things that exist have a cause

● it is impossible to go back forever looking for causes

● there must therefore have been a first cause, that was not caused itself

● Allah is the first cause as Allah is without cause and requires no explanation for His existence.

*The universe – the
work of Allah*

There are other possible arguments that could be put forward to demonstrate the fact of Allah's existence. For example, the fact that ever since the beginning of human history people have claimed to have experienced Allah may indicate the reality of Allah's presence in the universe.

Similarly, the world in which we live appears well ordered, as it sits in its orbit around the sun. Maybe the conditions for life on planet earth have been designed especially. If so there must have been a designer. This designer must have been Allah, the only power capable of such wonders.

In conclusion, the very fact that human beings have a sense of right and wrong and an understanding of what is meant by right and wrong must have come from somewhere. As children we have all made mistakes and have been guided by our parents – we have all been taught the correct way to behave. It is argued that this teaching and guidance must have come from Allah, the ultimate law giver and moral guide of all.

Learning about religion

❶ Why are Muslims in no doubt that Allah exists?

❷ Working with a partner, evaluate the strengths and weaknesses of the arguments discussed in this unit. Do they convince you of Allah's existence?

Learning from religion

❶ Do you think that there is evidence in the universe to suggest that Allah exists? What would you point to in order to convince someone of the reality of the existence of Allah?

❷ Is it bound to be the case that the nature and existence of Allah is always going to be beyond human imagination and understanding? Does it really matter? What reasons would you give for your answer?

Glossary

Abd servant

Adhan the call to prayer

Akhirah belief in life after death

Allah God

Angel messenger from Allah, visible under certain conditions

Belief firm opinion, acceptance without doubt

Blasphemy acting or speaking disrespectfully about Allah

CE Common Era

Du'a personal prayer or supplication

Faith the courage to accept the challenges of belief

Hadiths sayings and traditions of Muhammad (pbuh)

Hajj annual pilgrimage to Makkah

Hajji name given to a Muslim man who has performed Hajj

Hajjah name given to a Muslim woman who has performed Hajj

Halal allowed

Hijab covering cloak worn by Muslim women

Ibadah worship, being a servant of God

Id-ul-Adha feast of sacrifice, ends the Hajj

Id-ul-Fitr feast to break the fast

Ihram state of religious 'separation' or purity

Imam a teacher or leader

Injil the revelation given to 'Isa (Jesus)

Islam submission to Allah

Istjfaa calling to prophethood

Jihad striving, holy war in defence of Allah's will

Jinn elemental spirit

Ka'bah the 'Cube', shrine of Allah in Makkah

Kalimah Tayyibah the last words spoken by a Muslim before dying

Khalifah deputy for Allah

Khitan circumcision

Khutbah sermon

Madrasah school

Mihrab niche indicating the direction of Makkah

Minaret tower from which the call to prayer is given

Minbar pulpit for giving Friday sermons

Mosque place for communal prayer and activities

Muslims followers of Islam

Pbuh 'Peace be upon him' (said of the prophets)

Prophets holy people, through whom Allah has revealed something of himself

Qur'an the Revealed Book

Ramadan the month of fasting

Risalah prophecy

Sahifah of Ibrahim scrolls of Abraham and Moses

Salah ritual prayer five times daily

Sawm fasting from sunrise to sunset

Shahadah declaration of faith

Shaytan the Devil

Shirk sin of associating anything with Allah

Surah a chapter in the Qur'an

Tawhid the doctrine of the one-ness of Allah

Tawrah the revelation given to Musa (Moses) (pbuh)

Trust belief in the reliability or truth of something

Ummah the 'family' of Islam

Wudu ritual washing before prayer

Zabur the revelation given to Dawud (David) (pbuh)

Zakah giving of one-fortieth of savings for God's service

Places

Arafat Mount of Mercy, where Adam (pbuh) and Eve met after God forgave their sin

Jabal-un-Nur the Mountain of Light, where Muhammad (pbuh) regularly prayed in isolation in a cave

Makkah city of Ka'bah shrine, Muhammad's (pbuh) birthplace

Mina place of stoning the Devil on Hajj

Safa and **Marwah** places where Hajar searched for water

People

Abu Talib uncle of Muhammad (pbuh) who adopted him

Adam the first created man

Dawud the prophet David (pbuh), king of Israel

Fatimah daughter of Muhammad (pbuh)

Hajar wife of Ibrahim (pbuh)

Ibrahim Abraham, the 'father' of Jews and Arabs, and 'friend of God'

'Isa the prophet Jesus, worshipped by Christians

Isma'il the prophet Ishmael, son of Abraham

Jibril (Gabriel) the angel who transmitted revelations to Muhammad (pbuh)

Khadijah first wife of Muhammad (pbuh)

Muhammad the last and greatest of the prophets, to whom Allah revealed the Qu'ran

Musa the prophet Moses

Shaytan Satan, the devil, the chief Jinn

Suleiman the prophet Solomon, son of Dawud (David) (pbuh)

Index